Lecture Notes in Computer Science   13731

Kejiang Ye · Liang-Jie Zhang (Eds.)

Cloud Computing – CLOUD 2022

15th International Conference
Held as Part of the Services Conference Federation, SCF 2022
Honolulu, HI, USA, December 10–14, 2022
Proceedings

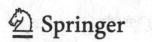
Springer

Editors
Kejiang Ye
Shenzhen Institutes of Advanced Technology
Chinese Academy of Sciences
Beijing, China

Liang-Jie Zhang ⓘ
Kingdee International Software
Group Co., Ltd.
Shenzhen, China

ISSN 0302-9743   ISSN 1611-3349 (electronic)
Lecture Notes in Computer Science
ISBN 978-3-031-23497-2   ISBN 978-3-031-23498-9 (eBook)
https://doi.org/10.1007/978-3-031-23498-9

This Springer imprint is published by the registered company Springer Nature Switzerland AG
The registered company address is: Gewerbestrasse 11, 6330 Cham, Switzerland

Preface

Being the first conference dedicated to cloud computing, the International Conference on Cloud Computing (CLOUD) has been a prime international forum for both researchers and industry practitioners to exchange the latest fundamental advances in the state of the art and practice of cloud computing, to identify emerging research topics, and to define the future of cloud computing. All topics related to cloud computing align with the theme of CLOUD.

CLOUD 2022 was one of the events of the Services Conference Federation event (SCF2022), which had the following 10 collocated service-oriented sister conferences: the International Conference on Web Services (ICWS 2022), the International Conference on Cloud Computing (CLOUD 2022), the International Conference on Services Computing (SCC 2022), the International Conference on Big Data (BigData 2022), the International Conference on AI & Mobile Services (AIMS 2022), the International Conference on Metaverse (METAVERSE 2022), the International Conference on Internet of Things (ICIOT 2022), the International Conference on Cognitive Computing (ICCC 2022), the International Conference on Edge Computing (EDGE 2022), and the International Conference on Blockchain (ICBC 2022).

This volume presents the papers accepted at (CLOUD 2022), Each paper was reviewed by three independent members of the Program Committee. After carefully evaluating their originality and quality, 9 papers are accepted.

We are pleased to thank the authors whose submissions and participation made this conference possible. We also want to express our thanks to the Program Committee members, for their dedication in helping to organize the conference and review the submissions.

We would like to thank operation team members Jing Zeng, Yishuang Ning and Sheng He for their excellent work in organizing this conference.

December 2022

Kejiang Ye
Liang-Jie Zhang

Organization

Services Conference Federation (SCF 2022)

General Chairs

Ali Arsanjani   Cloud Partner Engineering, Google, USA
Wu Chou   Vice President-Artificial Intelligence & Software
     at Essenlix Corporation, USA

Coordinating Program Chair

Liang-Jie Zhang   Kingdee International Software Group, China

CFO and International Affairs Chair

Min Luo   Georgia Tech, USA

Operation Committee

Jing Zeng   China Gridcom, China
Yishuang Ning   Tsinghua University, China
Sheng He   Tsinghua University, China

Steering Committee

Calton Pu   Georgia Tech, USA
Liang-Jie Zhang   Kingdee International Software Group, China

CLOUD 2022

Program Chair

Kejiang Ye   Shenzhen Institutes of Advanced Technology,
     Chinese Academy of Sciences, China

Program Committee

Gerald Baumgartner   Louisiana State University, USA
Jingshu Chen   Oakland University, USA

Krishna Kant	Temple University, USA
Yao Liu	Rutgers University, USA
Sanjay Patel	KSV, India
Rkn Sai Krishna	Teradata India, India
Ruediger Schulze	IBM Germany Research & Development, Germany
Jun Shen	University of Wollongong, Australia
Byung Chul Tak	Kyungpook National University, South Korea
Nan Wang	Heilongjiang University, China
Yingwei Wang	University of Prince Edward Island, Canada
Yuehua Wang	Texas A&M University – Commerce, USA
Hailu Xu	California State University, USA
Feng Yan	University of Nevada, USA
Ming Zhao	Arizona State University, USA

Services Society

The Services Society (S2) is a non-profit professional organization that was created to promote worldwide research and technical collaboration in services innovations among academia and industrial professionals. Its members are volunteers from industry and academia with common interests. S2 is registered in the USA as a "501(c) organization", which means that it is an American tax-exempt nonprofit organization. S2 collaborates with other professional organizations to sponsor or co-sponsor conferences and to promote an effective services curriculum in colleges and universities. S2 initiates and promotes a "Services University" program worldwide to bridge the gap between industrial needs and university instruction.

The Services Society has formed Special Interest Groups (SIGs) to support technology- and domain-specific professional activities:

- Special Interest Group on Web Services (SIG-WS)
- Special Interest Group on Services Computing (SIG-SC)
- Special Interest Group on Services Industry (SIG-SI)
- Special Interest Group on Big Data (SIG-BD)
- Special Interest Group on Cloud Computing (SIG-CLOUD)
- Special Interest Group on Artificial Intelligence (SIG-AI)
- Special Interest Group on Edge Computing (SIG-EC)
- Special Interest Group on Cognitive Computing (SIG-CC)
- Special Interest Group on Blockchain (SIG-BC)
- Special Interest Group on Internet of Things (SIG-IOT)
- Special Interest Group on Metaverse (SIG-Metaverse)

Services Conference Federation (SCF)

As the founding member of SCF, the first International Conference on Web Services (ICWS) was held in June 2003 in Las Vegas, USA. The First International Conference on Web Services - Europe 2003 (ICWS-Europe'03) was held in Germany in October 2003. ICWS-Europe'03 was an extended event of the 2003 International Conference on Web Services (ICWS 2003) in Europe. In 2004 ICWS-Europe changed to the European Conference on Web Services (ECOWS), which was held in Erfurt, Germany.

SCF 2019 was held successfully during June 25–30, 2019 in San Diego, USA. Affected by COVID-19, SCF 2020 was held online successfully during September 18–20, 2020, and SCF 2021 was held virtually during December 10–14, 2021.

Celebrating its 20-year birthday, the 2022 Services Conference Federation (SCF 2022, www.icws.org) was a hybrid conference with a physical onsite in Honolulu, Hawaii, USA, satellite sessions in Shenzhen, Guangdong, China, and also online sessions for those who could not attend onsite. All virtual conference presentations were given via prerecorded videos in December 10–14, 2022 through the BigMarker Video Broadcasting Platform: https://www.bigmarker.com/series/services-conference-federati/series_summit

Just like SCF 2022, SCF 2023 will most likely be a hybrid conference with physical onsite and virtual sessions online, it will be held in September 2023.

To present a new format and to improve the impact of the conference, we are also planning an Automatic Webinar which will be presented by experts in various fields. All the invited talks will be given via prerecorded videos and will be broadcast in a live-like format recursively by two session channels during the conference period. Each invited talk will be converted into an on-demand webinar right after the conference.

In the past 19 years, the ICWS community has expanded from Web engineering innovations to scientific research for the whole services industry. Service delivery platforms have been expanded to mobile platforms, the Internet of Things, cloud computing, and edge computing. The services ecosystem has been enabled gradually, with value added and intelligence embedded through enabling technologies such as Big Data, artificial intelligence, and cognitive computing. In the coming years, all transactions involving multiple parties will be transformed to blockchain.

Based on technology trends and best practices in the field, the Services Conference Federation (SCF) will continue to serve as a forum for all services-related conferences. SCF 2022 defined the future of the new ABCDE (AI, Blockchain, Cloud, Big Data & IOT). We are very proud to announce that SCF 2023's 10 colocated theme topic conferences will all center around "services", while each will focus on exploring different themes (Web-based services, cloud-based services, Big Data-based services, services innovation lifecycles, AI-driven ubiquitous services, blockchain-driven trust service ecosystems, Metaverse services and applications, and emerging service-oriented technologies).

The 10 colocated SCF 2023 conferences will be sponsored by the Services Society, the world-leading not-for-profit organization dedicated to serving more than 30,000 services computing researchers and practitioners worldwide. A bigger platform means bigger opportunities for all volunteers, authors, and participants. Meanwhile, Springer will provide sponsorship for Best Paper Awards. All 10 conference proceedings of SCF 2023 will be published by Springer, and to date the SCF proceedings have been indexed in the ISI Conference Proceedings Citation Index (included in the Web of Science), the Engineering Index EI (Compendex and Inspec databases), DBLP, Google Scholar, IO-Port, MathSciNet, Scopus, and ZbMath.

SCF 2023 will continue to leverage the invented Conference Blockchain Model (CBM) to innovate the organizing practices for all 10 conferences. Senior researchers in the field are welcome to submit proposals to serve as CBM ambassadors for individual conferences.

SCF 2023 Events

The 2023 edition of the Services Conference Federation (SCF) will include 10 service-oriented conferences: ICWS, CLOUD, SCC, BigData Congress, AIMS, METAVERSE, ICIOT, EDGE, ICCC and ICBC.

The 2023 International Conference on Web Services (ICWS 2023, http://icws.org/2023) will be the flagship theme-topic conference for Web-centric services, enabling technologies and applications.

The 2023 International Conference on Cloud Computing (CLOUD 2023, http://thecloudcomputing.org/2023) will be the flagship theme-topic conference for resource sharing, utility-like usage models, IaaS, PaaS, and SaaS.

The 2023 International Conference on Big Data (BigData 2023, http://bigdatacongress.org/2023) will be the theme-topic conference for data sourcing, data processing, data analysis, data-driven decision-making, and data-centric applications.

The 2023 International Conference on Services Computing (SCC 2023, http://thescc.org/2023) will be the flagship theme-topic conference for leveraging the latest computing technologies to design, develop, deploy, operate, manage, modernize, and redesign business services.

The 2023 International Conference on AI & Mobile Services (AIMS 2023, http://ai1000.org/2023) will be a theme-topic conference for artificial intelligence, neural networks, machine learning, training data sets, AI scenarios, AI delivery channels, and AI supporting infrastructures, as well as mobile Internet services. AIMS will bring AI to mobile devices and other channels.

The 2023 International Conference on Metaverse (Metaverse 2023, http://www.metaverse1000.org/2023) will focus on innovations of the services industry, including financial services, education services, transportation services, energy services, government services, manufacturing services, consulting services, and other industry services.

The 2023 International Conference on Cognitive Computing (ICCC 2023, http://thecognitivecomputing.org/2023) will focus on leveraging the latest computing technologies to simulate, model, implement, and realize cognitive sensing and brain operating systems.

The 2023 International Conference on Internet of Things (ICIOT 2023, http://iciot.org/2023) will focus on the science, technology, and applications of IOT device innovations as well as IOT services in various solution scenarios.

The 2023 International Conference on Edge Computing (EDGE 2023, http://theedgecomputing.org/2023) will be a theme-topic conference for leveraging the latest computing technologies to enable localized device connections, edge gateways, edge applications, edge-cloud interactions, edge-user experiences, and edge business models.

The 2023 International Conference on Blockchain (ICBC 2023, http://blockchain1000.org/2023) will concentrate on all aspects of blockchain, including digital currencies, distributed application development, industry-specific blockchains, public blockchains, community blockchains, private blockchains, blockchain-based services, and enabling technologies.

Contents

Performance Evaluation of Modified Best First Decreasing Algorithms for Dynamic Virtual Machine Placement in Cloud Computing

Joseph Akinwumi[1,2]([✉]) [iD] and Ibrahim Adeyanju[2] [iD]

[1] Department of Computer Engineering, Afe Babalola University, Ado-Ekiti, Nigeria
jakinwumi@abuad.edu.ng
[2] Department of Computer Engineering, Federal University, Oye-Ekiti, Nigeria

Abstract. Cloud computing has become the popular choice in developing countries such as Nigeria where access to high performance computing facilities is inadequate. Individuals, organizations and institutions in need of high performance computing facilities can subscribe to cloud computing facilities on a pay-as-you-go basis. Whenever a customer requests for cloud computing services, there is a problem of allocating virtual machines for such services on available physical machines while minimizing energy consumption and carbon-dioxide emission, as well as maximizing resource utilization. The Modified Best First Decreasing(MBFD) algorithm is a baseline algorithm for evaluating the performance of virtual machine placement algorithms in cloud computing. This research carries out a performance evaluation of the MBFD algorithms in the CloudSim 3.0.3 simulator under three different configurations A, B and C. Configuration A has fewer processor resources than configuration B which has fewer processor resources than configuration C. CloudSim 3.0.3 is installed in Eclipse Integrated Development Environment on a Laptop with two Intel Celeron Processors at 1.60 GHz each and 4 GB memory. Configurations B and C have lower energy consumption and faster computation time compared to configuration A. The lowest average energy consumption is 101.97 KWh and standard deviation of 8.63 KWh when Local Regression Robust with minimum utilization heuristic algorithm was executed under configuration B. The fastest average computation time is 0.21898 s for static threshold with minimum utilization heuristic algorithm under configuration B. This work recommends evaluating the adaptive heuristics on real-life cloud computing testbed to further validate the results.

Keywords: Virtual machine placement · Infrastructure as a service · Energy consumption · Cloud computing

1 Introduction

Cloud computing has become the popular choice in developing countries such as Nigeria where access to high performance computing facilities is inadequate. The virtual machine placement problem is the mapping of virtual machines to host machines so as to reduce

K. Ye and L.-J. Zhang (Eds.): CLOUD 2022, LNCS 13731, pp. 1–12, 2022.
https://doi.org/10.1007/978-3-031-23498-9_1

energy consumption and increase resource utilization. Cloud computing services include Software as a Service (SaaS), Platform as a Service (PaaS) and Infrastructure as a Service (IaaS) [1]. Applications are provided at a fee but hosted on third-party system and accessed via the Internet and the web in the Software as a Service model. Google Apps, Dropbox and Gmail are examples of SaaS. Development platforms are made available to developers for a fee and are hosted by third-parties in Platform as a Service. Examples of PaaS are Amazon Web Service Elastic Beanstalk, Heroku and Windows Azure. In IaaS, hardware and operating systems resources to host whatever an organization wants to implement are provided. IaaS is hosted by third-party for a fee. Examples of IaaS are Amazon Web Services, Rackspace and Google Compute Engine.

This paper studies the problem of dynamic virtual machine placement by varying the host configurations. The problem of dynamic virtual machine placement was studied by (2) and a bound on the competitive ratio was determined. However, the authors did not consider the effect of different host configurations including processor speeds, memory, bandwidth and storage space. Furthermore, no previous work studied the effect of varying host configuration on energy consumption and computation time. This work varies the host configuration and determines which configuration gives the lowest energy consumption and fastest computation time.

The remaining sections are related work, system model, performance evaluation, discussion, conclusion and recommendations. The related work section discusses previous research work in dynamic virtual machine placement while the system model describes dynamic virtual machine placement problem. Performance evaluation discusses the implementation tools, experimental setup and results. Discussion section explains the results while conclusion and recommendations draw conclusion and recommends future work.

2 Related Work

Dynamic virtual machine (VM) placement was studied by [2–16]. A bound on the competitive ratio was determined and several adaptive heuristics were proposed in [2]. In [15], a regression based method for predicting resource utilization of VMs and hosts based on historical data was proposed. This method improves energy efficiency. A Discrete-Time Markov Chain (DTMC) model was used to predict resource usage and a multi-objective artificial bee colony algorithm was used to balance energy consumption and resource wastage in [16]. The proposed approach improves energy consumption.

The dynamic virtual machine placement problem was solved using Integer Linear Programming to obtain the most energy efficient way of placing the VMs under fluctuating workloads [5]. A real virtualized data center testbed was used to evaluate the design. The problem of optimal VM placement and migration to minimize resource usage and power consumption was studied by [3]. An optimization problem was formulated as a joint multiple objective function and solved using convex optimization. Under dynamic workloads, uncertainty, and a changing number of VMs, [13] proposed power-aware VM consolidation based on integral estimation optimal beam search considering four types of resources: CPU, memory, network throughput and storage throughput. Experiments showed the proposed method was efficient in usage of cloud resources.

In [4], a VM placement approach was presented that aims at minimizing the total energy of a data center. The Ant Colony Optimization algorithm was used to solve the problem. In [7], the Unified Ant Colony System was applied to solve the dynamic virtual machine placement problem of using fewest servers to host the virtual machines. The UACS was competitive compared to traditional heuristic, probabilistic, and other ACS based algorithms. In [10], a parallel ant colony optimization algorithm was proposed to solve the dynamic virtual machine placement problem. The solution obtained was comparable to or superior to previous techniques.

Genetic algorithm was used to solve the dynamic virtual machine placement problem so as to minimize underutilization and overutilization scenarios [6]. Cloudsim was used to evaluate the virtual machine placement algorithm. The virtual machine placement problem was solved using a memetic algorithm which combines partheno-genetic algorithm with multi-player random evolutionary game theory [9]. The proposed algorithm outperforms other techniques. A new evolutionary meta-heuristic based on island population model was used to approximate the pareto optimal set of VM placement in [14]. Traces from real Google cluster showed that the approach performed better than similar methods.

A dynamic virtual machine placement using statistical mathematic framework to minimize the number of active nodes so as to save energy was proposed in [8]. Extensive evaluations were conducted in a simulation environment. Side attack channels were mitigated by using greedy and previously selected server first policy in [11]. A normalization-based VM consolidation (NVMC) strategy which placed virtual machines in an online manner and minimizes energy consumption, SLA violations and number of VM migrations, was proposed in [12]. NVMC outperforms other famous approaches.

3 System Model

The system model consists of N heterogeneous physical nodes each characterized by CPU performance in Millions Instructions Per Seconds (MIPS), Random Access Memory (RAM) and Network Bandwidth. The environment is Infrastructure As A Service (IAAS) with network attached storage provided. Also, M virtual machine(VM) requests for processing power (CPU), RAM and network bandwidth are made by multiple users from the physical nodes. The workload is a mixture of high performance computing (hpc) and web applications.

The dynamic VM consolidation problem is divided in four parts: (1) deciding when a host is overloaded so that one or more VMs is migrated from this host. (2) deciding when a host is underloaded so that all VMs on the host can be migrated and the host is switched to sleep mode (3) choosing VMs to be migrated from the overloaded host (4) computing a new placement of VMs for the overloaded and underloaded hosts.

The virtual machine placement can be viewed as an NP-hard bin packing problem which can be solved using the Modified Best Fit Decreasing(MBFD) algorithm with no more than 11/9.OPT + 1 bins (OPT is the number of bins of the optimal solution) [2]. The MBFD algorithm sorts all the VMs in decreasing order of their current CPU utilizations and allocate each VM to a host with the least increase in power consumption as a result of the allocation. The MBFD algorithm is described in Algorithm 1.

Algorithm 1:Modified Best Fit Decreasing (MBFD) [2]
---
1 Input: hostList, vmList Output: allocation of VMs
2 vmList.sortDecreasingUtilization()
3 foreach vm in vmList do
4   minPower←MAX
5   allocatedHost←NULL
6   foreachhost in hostList do
7   if host has enough resources for vm then
8   power←estimatePower(host, vm)
9   if power < minPower then
10   allocatedHost←host
11   minPower←power
12   if allocatedHost ≠ NULL then
13   allocation.add(vm, allocatedHost)
14 return allocation

---

4 Performance Evaluation

4.1 Implementation Tools

This work is focused on placement of virtual machine requests on physical machines. CloudSim 3.0.3 simulator [2] was chosen because experimentation in real cloud environment is not advisable and there is need for reproducibility of cloud computing experiments. CloudSim is a discrete event simulator written in Java, it is open source and extensible. CloudSim was installed in the Eclipse Integrated Development Environment (IDE) on a Laptop Computer hardware with two Intel Celeron (N3060) Processors each having 1.60 GHz speed and 4 GB Memory.

The input to the CloudSim simulator is the Planetlab [17] workload. Planetlab is a global initiative for research in distributed computing. It has physical nodes worldwide that run several co-located but isolated user tasks (slices) using virtualization. The PlanetLab workload contains CPU resource requests with each file having 288 requests. There are over 1000 files for each day. Each file represents a VM. There are 800 hosts in each PlanetLab workload. The mean and range of each workload is as shown in Table 1. The mean for the five randomly selected workloads is 11.25 and the standard deviation is 0.71. Each workload has CPU requests ranging from 0 to 99.

Table 1. Summary of PlanetLab Workload

Planetlab Workload	Mean CPU request	Range
2011/03/03	12.31	99
2011/03/09	10.70	99
2011/03/25	10.56	99
2011/04/09	11.12	99
2011/04/12	11.54	99

The baseline algorithms implemented in CloudSim include variants of Modified Best First Decreasing such as [2]: Interquartile Range VM overload detection and Minimum utilization VM selection policy (Iqr_Mu); Local Regression VM overload detection and Minimum utilization VM selection policy (LrMu); Robust Local Regression VM overload detection and Minimum Utilization VM selection policy (LrrMu); Static Threshold VM overload detection and Minimum Utilization selection policy (Thr_Mu). The InterQuartile Range(Iqr) is a method for setting adaptive upper utilization threshold based on a robust test statistic. IQR is the difference between the third and first Quartiles, IQR = Q3–Q1. Local regression (Lr) is fitting simple models to localized subsets of data to build-up a curve that approximates the original data. A trend polynomial is fit to the last k observations of the CPU utilization. Robust local regression (Lrr) is less vulnerable to outliers in heavy-tailed distribution.

4.2 Experimental Setup on CloudSim

The configurations of virtual machine (VM) and host/physical machines PM in CloudSim 3.0.3 is given in Table 2 and Table 3 respectively. There are four types of VMs and two types of PMs. The four types of VMs have VM processor speed, VM_MIPS of 2500, 2000, 1000 and 500 million instructions per seconds (MIPS). The virtual machine memory, VM_RAM were 870, 1740, 1740, 613 Mega Bytes (MB).

Table 2. Virtual machine configuration (as available in CloudSim)

VM_TYPES	VM_MIPS (MIPS)	VM_RAM (MB)	VM_BW (Kbits/sec)	VM_SIZE (MB)
TYPE 1	2500	870	100000	2500
TYPE 2	2000	1740	100000	2500
TYPE 3	1000	1740	100000	2500
TYPE 4	500	613	100000	2500

Table 3. Physical machine configuration A, B and C (as available in CloudSim)

HOST_TYPE	HOST_MIPS A(MHz)	HOST_MIPS B(MHz)	HOST_MIPS C(MHz)	HOST_RAM (MB)	HOST_BW (KBits/sec)	HOST_STORAGE (Byte)
HOST_TYPE 1	1860	1860	3720	4096	1000	1000000
HOST_TYPE 2	2660	5320	5320	4096	1000	1000000

The virtual machine bandwidth, VM_BW is 100 Mbits/sec and the virtual machine size, VM_SIZE is 2500 MB. The configurations of the physical machines in Experiment A, B and C are given in Table 3. In experiment A, the processor speeds were 1860 MIPS for HOST_TYPE 1 and 2660 MIPS for HOST_TYPE 2. The processor speeds were increased from 1860, 2660 to 1860, 5320 in experiment B.. The processor speeds were increased from 1860, 2660 to 3720, 5320 in experiment C. In all experiments, the memory of the host physical machine, HOST_RAM was 4096 MB while the host bandwidth, HOST_BW was 1000000 Bits/sec. The host storage space, HOST_STORAGE, was 1000000 Byte in all experiments.

4.3 Results from Experimentation with Modified Best First Decreasing Algorithms

In experiment A, B and C, variants of MBFD algorithm were executed namely: Iqr_Mu; LrMu; LrrMu; Thr_Mu. [2] The workload is obtained from Planetlab. The Energy Consumption, computation time and number of virtual machines are shown in Table 4.

The LrMu and LrrMU heuristic algorithm have the minimum energy consumption.. The heuristic algorithm with the highest energy consumption is the ThrMu. The mean Energy consumption of each heuristic algorithm is 197.28 for IqrMu, 168.56 for LrMu, 168.568 for LrrMu and 199.1 for ThrMu. The corresponding standard deviation is 16.47 for IqrMu, 14.80 for LrMu, 14.80 for LrrMu and 16.23 for ThrMu.

The mean energy consumption for each day is 189.86 for day 2011/03/03, 166.56 for day 2011/03/09, 175.64 for day 2011/03/25, 206.9 for day 2011/04/09 and 177.93 for day 2011/04/12. The corresponding standard deviation for each day is 18.06 for day 2011/03/03, 17.15 for day 2011/03/09, 15.33 for day 2011/03/25, 18.52 for day 2011/04/09 and 16.56 for day 2011/04/12.

Table 4. Energy Consumption for MBFD heuristics in Experiment A

Energy Consumption (KWh) and Computation time (sec)	Number of VMs	IqrMu (KWh)	IqrMu (sec)	LrMU (KWh)	LrMU (sec)	LrrMu (KWh)	LrrMu (sec)	ThrMu (KWh)	ThrMu (sec)
2011/03/03	1052	204.2	0.632	174.2	0.501	174.2	0.590	206.7	0.383
2011/03/09	1061	180.2	0.526	151.7	0.389	151.7	0.460	182.6	0.299
2011/03/25	1078	188.4	0.565	162.4	0.469	162.4	0.531	189.4	0.334
2011/04/09	1358	222.4	0.789	190.9	0.646	190.9	0.728	223.5	0.427
2011/04/12	1054	191.3	0.553	163.6	0.477	163.6	0.539	193.2	0.332

The computation time for the heuristic algorithms IqrMu, LrMu, LrrMu, ThrMu for experiment A are shown in Table 4. The mean for IqrMu is 0.613068, for LrMu is 0.496496, LrrMu is 0.569394 and for ThrMu is 0.355008. The standard deviation for the heuristic algorithms are 0.1060313 for IqrMu, 0.093591 for LrMu, 0.099785 for LrrMu and 0.050259 for ThrMu.

The energy consumption and computation time for MBFD heuristics for experiment B is shown in Table 5. The Local Regression and Local Regression Robust algorithms have lowest energy consumption The results for Iqr_Mu is slightly lower than the results for Thr_Mu. The heuristic algorithm with the highest energy consumption is the ThrMu. The mean Energy Consumption for each heuristic algorithm is 116.26 for IqrMu, 102.10 for LrMu, 101.97 for LrrMu and 118.46 for ThrMu. The standard deviation for each heuristic algorithm is 8.13 for IqrMu, 8.86 for LrMu, 8.63 for LrrMu and 9.44 for ThrMu.

Table 5. Energy Consumption for MBFD heuristics in Experiment B

Energy Consumption (KWh) and Computation time (sec)	IqrMu (KWh)	IqrMu (sec)	LrMu (KWh)	LrMu (sec)	LrrMu (KWh)	LrrMu (sec)	ThrMu (KWh)	ThrMu (sec)
2011/03/03	118.4	0.4129	105.8	0.3421	105.8	0.3553	122.4	0.2269
2011/03/09	105.4	0.3820	91.4	0.2737	91.4	0.2872	107.8	0.1858
2011/03/25	112.0	0.3819	97.9	0.3107	97.9	0.3995	113.6	0.2068
2011/04/09	127.3	0.4998	114.9	0.4140	114.3	0.4916	132.5	0.2665
2011/04/12	118.2	0.3668	100.4	0.3090	100.4	0.3831	115.9	0.2089

The mean energy consumption for each workload is 113.11 for workload 2011/03/03, 99.01 for workload 2011/03/09, 105.37 for workload 2011/03/25, 122.25 for workload 2011/04/09 and 108.74 for workload 2011/04/12. The standard deviation for each workload is 8.56 for workload 2011/03/03, 8.84 for workload 2011/03/09, 8.64 for workload 2011/03/25, 9.08 for workload 2011/04/09 and 9.65 for workload 2011/04/12.

The computation time for the heuristic algorithms IqrMu, LrMu, LrrMu, ThrMu for experiment B are shown in Table 5. The mean for IqrMu is 0.408668, for LrMu is 0.329898, LrrMu is 0.383342 and for ThrMu is 0.21898. The standard deviation for the heuristic algorithms are 0.0536308 for IqrMu, 0.052908 for LrMu, 0.074203 for LrrMu and 0.030314 for ThrMu.

The energy consumption for MBFD heuristics for experiment B is shown in Table 6. The Local Regression algorithm has lowest energy. The results for Iqr_Mu is slightly lower than the results for Thr_Mu. The mean Energy Consumption for each of the heuristic algorithm is 114.52 for IqrMu, 102.36 for LrMu, 102.36 for LrrMu and 117.89 for ThrMu. The standard deviation for each of the heuristic algorithm is 8.11 for IqrMu, 8.80 for LrMu, 8.80 for LrrMu and 9.23 for ThrMu.

The mean Energy Consumption for each workload is 113.02 for workload 2011/03/03, 99.14 for workload 2011/03/09, 105.73 for workload 2011/03/25, 122.19 for workload 2011/04/09 and 106.34 for workload 2011/04/12. The standard deviation for each day is 8.56 for workload 2011/03/03, 8.06 for workload 2011/03/09, 8.24 for workload 2011/03/25, 7.91 for workload 2011/04/09 and 7.85 for workload 2011/04/12.

The computation time for the heuristic algorithms IqrMu, LrMu, LrrMu, ThrMu for experiment C are shown in Table 6. The mean for IqrMu is 0.399818, for LrMu is

Table 6. Energy consumption for MBFD heuristics in Experiment C

Energy Consumption (KWh) and computation time (sec)	IqrMu (KWh)	IqrMu (sec)	LrMU (KWh)	LrMu (sec)	LrrMu (KWh)	LrrMu (sec)	ThrMu (KWh)	ThrMu (sec)
2011/03/03	117.5	0.4192	105.9	0.3467	105.9	0.3572	122.9	0.2290
2011/03/09	105.2	0.3501	92.2	0.2815	92.2	0.3033	107.0	0.1834
2011/03/25	111.7	0.3759	98.6	0.3176	98.6	0.3326	114.0	0.2142
2011/04/09	126.8	0.4814	115.5	0.4044	115.5	0.4468	131.0	0.2628
2011/04/12	111.6	0.3726	99.6	0.3333	99.6	0.3465	114.6	0.2259

0.336696, LrrMu is 0.357278 and for ThrMu is 0.223062. The standard deviation for the heuristic algorithms are 0.0519843 for IqrMu, 0.044988 for LrMu, 0.053963 for LrrMu and 0.028621 for ThrMu.

4.4 Discussions

The energy consumption for each of configurations B and C is lower than the corresponding energy consumption for configuration A. The processor speeds of the configuration B are lower than configuration C. The Local Regression Algorithm has the lowest energy consumption in each of the experiments. Figure 1 shows the energy consumption of heuristic algorithm IqrMu in three different configurations.

The configuration C has the lowest energy consumption of all the configurations. The mean energy consumption of heuristic algorithm IqrMu in configuration A is 197.28, 116.26 for configuration B and 114.52 for configuration C. The standard deviation for heuristic algorithm IqrMu is 16.46 for configuration A, 8.13 for configuration B and 8.11 for configuration C.

The mean energy consumption for heuristic algorithm IqrMu executed on the three configurations is 146.69 for workload 2011/03/03, 130.26 for workload 2011/03/09, 137.36 for workload 2011/03/25, 158.79 for workload 2011/04/09 and 140.34 for workload 2011/04/12. The standard deviation for heuristic algorithm IqrMu executed on the three configurations is 49.82 for workload 2011/03/03, 43.22 for workload 2011/03/09, 44.20 for workload 2011/03/25, 55.05 for workload 2011/04/09 and 44.23 for workload 2011/04/12.

Figure 1 shows the chart of the energy consumption of heuristic algorithm LrMu in three different configurations. The configuration C has the lowest energy consumption of all the configurations. The mean energy consumption of heuristic algorithm LrMu in configuration A is 168.56, 102.10 for configuration B and 102.36 for configuration C. The standard deviation for heuristic algorithm LrMu is 14.80 for configuration A, 8.85 for configuration B and 8.79 for configuration C.

The mean energy consumption for heuristic algorithm LrMu executed on the three configurations is 128.64 for workload 2011/03/03, 111.77 for workload 2011/03/09,

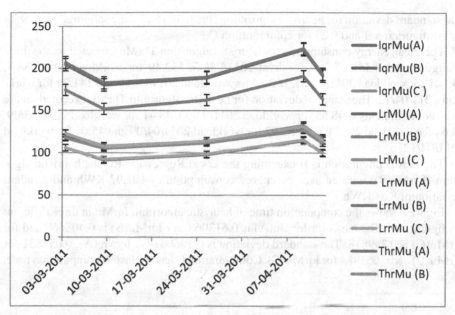

Fig. 1. Chart of energy consumption comparing IqrMu, LrMu, LrrMu and ThrMU each in configurations A, B and C

119.63 for workload 2011/03/25, 140.43 for workload 2011/04/09 and 121.21 for workload 2011/04/12. The standard deviation for heuristic algorithm LrMu executed on the three configurations is 39.48 for workload 2011/03/03, 34.61 for workload 2011/03/09, 37.00 for workload 2011/03/25, 43.68 for workload 2011/04/09 and 36.71 for workload 2011/04/12.

Figure 1 shows the chart of the energy consumption of heuristic algorithm LrrMu in three different configurations. The configuration C has the lowest energy consumption of all the configurations. The mean energy consumption of heuristic algorithm LrrMu in configuration A is 168.57, 101.97 for configuration B and 102.36 for configuration C. The standard deviation for heuristic algorithm LrrMu is 14.80 for configuration A, 8.62 for configuration B and 8.80 for configuration C.

The mean energy consumption for heuristic algorithm LrrMu executed on the three configurations is 128.64 for workload 2011/03/03, 111.77 for workload 2011/03/09, 119.65 for workload 2011/03/25, 140.22 for workload 2011/04/09 and 121.21 for workload 2011/04/12. The standard deviation for heuristic algorithm LrrMu executed on the three configurations is 39.48 for workload 2011/03/03, 34.61 for workload 2011/03/09, 37.02 for workload 2011/03/25, 43.87 for workload 2011/04/09 and 36.71 for workload 2011/04/12.

Figure 1 shows the chart of the energy consumption of heuristic algorithm ThrMu in three different configurations. The configuration C has the lowest energy consumption of all the configurations. The mean energy consumption of heuristic algorithm ThrMu in configuration A is 199.1, 118.46 for configuration B and 117.89 for configuration C.

The standard deviation for heuristic algorithm ThrMu is 16.23 for configuration A, 9.44 for configuration B and 9.23 for configuration C.

The mean energy consumption for heuristic algorithm ThrMu executed on the three configurations is 150.67 for workload 2011/03/03, 132.49 for workload 2011/03/09, 139.01 for workload 2011/03/25, 162.34 for workload 2011/04/09 and 141.24 for workload 2011/04/12. The standard deviation for heuristic algorithm ThrMu executed on the three configurations is 48.55 for workload 2011/03/03, 43.41 for workload 2011/03/09, 43.64 for workload 2011/03/25, 52.97 for workload 2011/04/09 and 45.04 for workload 2011/04/12.

The best configuration is B executing the Local Regression Robust heuristic algorithm (LrrMu(B)) with an average energy consumption of 101.97 KWh and standard deviation of 8.63 KWh.

Figure 2 shows the computation time of heuristic algorithm IqrMu in three different configurations. The mean for IqrMu(A) is 0.613068, for IqrMu(B) is 0.408668 and for IqrMu(C) is 0.399818. The standard deviation is 0.106031 for IqrMu(A), 0.053631 for IqrMu(B) and 0.051984 for IqrMu(C). Configuration C has the fastest computation time.

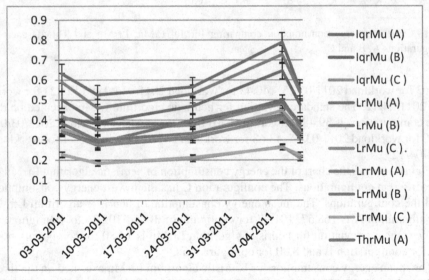

Fig. 2. Chart of computation time comparing IqrMu, LrMu, LrrMu and ThrMu in configurations A, B and C

Figure 2 shows the computation time of heuristic algorithm LrMu in three different configurations. The mean for LrMu(A) is 0.496496, for LrMu(B) is 0.3299 and for LrMu(C) is 0.3367. The standard deviation is 0.093591 for LrMu(A), 0.05291 for LrMu(B) and 0.04499 for LrMu(C). Configurations B and C has the fastest computation time.

Figure 2 shows the computation time of heuristic algorithm LrrMu in three different configurations. The mean for LrrMu(A) is 0.569394, for LrrMu(B) is 0.383342 and for LrrMu(C) is 0.357278. The standard deviation is 0.0997849 for LrrMu(A), 0.074203 for LrrMu(B) and 0.053963 for LrrMu(C). Configuration C has the fastest computation time.

Figure 2 shows the computation time of heuristic algorithm IqrMu in three different configurations. The mean for ThrMu(A) is 0.355008, for ThrMu(B) is 0.21898 and for ThrMu(C) is 0.223062. The standard deviation is 0.0502593 for ThrMu(A), 0.030314 for ThrMu(B) and 0.028621 for ThrMu(C). Configurations B and C has the fastest computation time. The fastest average computation time is 0.21898 s for ThrMu heuristic algorithm under configuration B.

ANOVA single factor was computed for energy consumption using each algorithm running in a configuration as a group. The p-value is less than 0.05 so the conclusion that at least one mean is different. The paired t-test was evaluated between the energy consumption of each algorithm in configurations B and C to test if the means are significantly different. The p-value is greater than 0.05 so the means are not different. Further, the means of LrMu in configuration A and LrrMu in configuration A, LrMu in configuration B and LrrMu in configuration B, LrMu in configuration C and LrrMu in configuration C respectively are not significantly different using the paired t test. Similar analyses were performed and results obtained for the computation time.

5 Conclusion and Recommendation

This work studied the best configuration for dynamic virtual machine placement while running some selected adaptive heuristics such as: IqrMu, LrMu, LrrMu, ThrMu. Configurations B and C have lower energy consumption and faster computation time compared to configuration A. The results are lowest average energy consumption of 101.97KWh and standard deviation of 8.63 KWh when Local Regression Robust with minimum utilization (LrrMu) heuristic algorithm was executed under configuration B. The fastest average computation time is 0.21898 s for static threshold with minimum utilization (ThrMu) heuristic algorithm under configuration B. Configuration B had a similar performance to configuration C except for LrrMu adaptive heuristic running on configuration B having a slower computation time than LrrMu on configuration C. These indicate that increasing the processor speed does not always result in lower energy consumption and faster computation time. This work recommends evaluating the adaptive heuristics on real-life cloud computing testbed to further validate the results.

References

1. Puthal, D., et al.: Cloud computing features, issues and challenges: a big picture. In: 2015 International Conference on Computational Intelligence and Networks, pp. 116–123 (2015)
2. Beloglazov, A., Buyya, R.: Optimal online deterministic algorithms and adaptive heuristics for energy and performance efficient dynamic consolidation of virtual machines in cloud data centers. Concurrency Comput.: Pract. Exp. **24**(13), 1397–1420 (2012)
3. Duong-Ba, T.,et al.: A dynamic virtual machine placement and migration scheme for data centers. IEEE Trans. Serv. Comput. **14**(2), 329–341 (2018)
4. Alharbi, F, et al.: Profile-based ant colony optimization for energy-efficient virtual machine placement. In: International Conference on Neural Information Processing, pp. 863–871. Springer Cham (2017). https://doi.org/10.1007/978-3-319-70087-8_88

5. Zhang, Z., Hsu, C.C., Chang, M.: Cool cloud: a practical dynamic virtual machine placement framework for energy aware data centers. In: 2015 IEEE 8th International Conference on Cloud Computing, pp. 758–765 (2015)
6. Mosa, A., Sakellariou, R.: Dynamic virtual machine placement considering CPU and memory resource requirements. In: 2019 IEEE 12th International Conference on Cloud Computing (CLOUD), pp. 196–198 (2019)
7. Liu, X.F., Zhan, Z.H., Zhang, J.: An energy aware unified ant colony system for dynamic virtual machine placement in cloud computing. Energies **10**(5), 609 (2017)
8. Zheng, X., Cai, Y.: Dynamic virtual machine placement for cloud computing environments. In: 2014 43rd International Conference on Parallel Processing Workshops, pp. 121–128 (2014)
9. Xiao, Z., Ming, Z.: A state based energy optimization framework for dynamic virtual machine placement. Data Knowl. Eng. **120**, 83–99 (2019)
10. Peake, J., Amos, M., Costen, N., Masala, G., Lloyd, H.: PACO-VMP: parallel ant colony optimization for virtual machine placement. Future Gener. Comput. Syst. **129**, 174–186 (2022)
11. Gali, A.M.R., Koduganti, V.R.: Dynamic and scalable virtual machine placement algorithm for mitigating side channel attacks in cloud computing. Materials Today (2021)
12. Khan, M. A.: An efficient energy-aware approach for dynamic VM consolidation on cloud platforms. Cluster Comput. **24**(4), 3293–3310 (2021). https://doi.org/10.1007/s10586-021-03341-0
13. Zharikov, E., Telenyk, S.: Performance analysis of dynamic virtual machine management method based on the power-aware integral estimation. Electronics **10**(21), 2581 (2021)
14. Torre, E., et al.: A dynamic evolutionary multi-objective virtual machine placement heuristic for cloud data centers. Inf. Softw. Technol. **128**, 106390 (2020)
15. Haghshenas, K., Mohammadi, S.: Prediction-based underutilized and destination host selection approaches for energy-efficient dynamic VM consolidation in data centers. J. Supercomput. **76**(12), 10240–10257 (2020). https://doi.org/10.1007/s11227-020-03248-4
16. Sayadnavard, M.H., Haghighat, A.T., Rahmani, A.M.: A multi-objective approach for energy-efficient and reliable dynamic VM consolidation in cloud data centers. Eng. Sci. Technol. Int. J. **26** (2022)
17. Eyraud-Dubois, L., Uznanski, P.: Point-to-point and congestion bandwidth estimation: experimental evaluation on PlanetLab data. In: IEEE International Parallel & Distributed Processing Symposium Workshops, pp. 89–96 (2014)

Towards an Efficient Client Selection System for Federated Learning

Guanyu Ding[1], Zhengxiong Li[2], Yusen Wu[3], Xiaokun Yang[4], Mehrdad Aliasgari[1], and Hailu Xu[1(✉)]

[1] Department of Computer Engineering and Computer Science,
California State University, Long Beach, USA
mehrdad.aliasgari@csulb.edu, hailu.xu@csulb.edu
[2] University of Colorado Denver, Denver, USA
zhengxiong.li@ucdenver.edu
[3] University of Miami, Coral Gables, USA
yxw1259@miami.edu
[4] University of Houston, Clear Lake, USA
yangxia@uhcl.edu

Abstract. Federated learning is a popular distributed machine learning model where a centralized server orchestrates many distributed clients to coordinate the completion of model training or evaluation without sharing private or local data. More and more modern data applications turn to federated learning models due to their scalability and privacy preservation. Selecting proper clients for model training and evaluation is a key issue for federated learning. Many existing works propose to optimize the client selection for a single application with various resource limitations for each client. However, they rarely focus on client selection for many heterogeneous applications that require various kinds of resources. In this paper, we propose FedPod, a novel system that can efficiently and instantly provide appropriate clients for different federated learning applications. By utilizing the real-time resource usage information and the estimated run-time resource requirements, FedPod can instantly provide an optimal available set of clients by adopting the best-fit policy. Experimental results show that it can provide accurate client selection decisions even with a large number of jobs, with achieving low latency in client selection.

Keywords: Federated learning · Task allocation · Client selection

1 Introduction

Model machine learning is moving both data collection and model training to the edge of the network, thus, to the huge volume of distributed edge devices (e.g., smartphones, autonomous vehicles, and wearable devices). Federated Learning (FL), a distributed optimization paradigm that enables a centralized node to organize a large number of client nodes to cooperatively complete the model training, has been drawing more and more attention to the current heavy-loaded

© The Author(s), under exclusive license to Springer Nature Switzerland AG 2022
K. Ye and L.-J. Zhang (Eds.): CLOUD 2022, LNCS 13731, pp. 13–21, 2022.
https://doi.org/10.1007/978-3-031-23498-9_2

data applications. In Federated Learning models, local data from distributed clients is not needed to be uploaded to the centralized server, thus the model can be distributed and trained in the local clients, reducing the network bandwidth overhead and privacy leaking concerns. After local clients perform a few iterations of training using local-update stochastic gradient descent (SGD), they only periodically send model updates to the centralized server for calculating a global statistical model [2,4].

While federated learning models have been widely explored in more data applications, client selection is a non-trivial problem when faced with heterogeneous device capabilities, characteristics of data, and run-time requirements of applications. Most of the previous work considers full client participation, which means all nodes participate in every training cycle [4,11]. However, full client participation wastes a lot of computation resources and brings huge overhead to all devices. Some research work selects only a fraction of clients to complete the several iterations of training cycles. However, partial client selection facing with more challenges such as the heterogeneity of the client's local data, various available computation resources, and communication bandwidths [12].

In this paper, we propose FedPod, a novel efficient client selection system for handling many heterogeneous federated learning applications. The key idea is FedPod can instantly collect the runtime performances and resource usage of each client and efficiently select the most appropriate set of clients for new applications at scale.

FedPod operates in two phases. The first phase is the runtime resource usage collection. FedPod builds many resource management trees based on a distributed hash table (DHT) [10], that can instantly collect the runtime performance and resource usages of each client. Among the tree, each client works as a leaf and sends their runtime performances to the tree root. Tree root orchestrates the following clients and gathers the resource usage of all clients. The second phase is the client selection for new applications. A tree root can estimate the workload of new federated learning applications and adopt a best-fit based policy to find the most proper set of available clients that can handle the specific application. In this phase, we design a resource usage model in the system for estimating the workload of data applications and organizing the resources of each client.

This paper makes the following contributions:

- An efficient client selection prototype named FedPod is presented that organize the selection of available clients in federated learning.
- FedPod adopts a best-fit based policy to select the proper set of clients for various types of federated learning applications.
- FedPod can collect the real-time resource usage information from clients and make decision based on the available resources of real-time details.

The rest of this paper is organized as follows: Sect. 2 details the functionality design and workflow of the system. Section 3 shows the initial evaluation results. We discuss the related works in Sect. 4 and conclude the future work in Sect. 5.

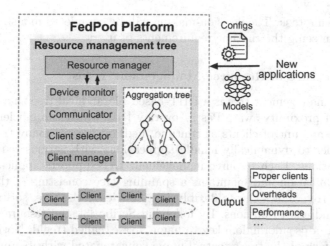

Fig. 1. The overview and functional components of FedPd.

2 Design

In this section, we introduce the design details of FedPod, which includes the system overview and the details of its functional components. We also outline the details of the workflow in the system.

2.1 Overview

Figure 1 shows the architecture of the FedPod system. FedPod is built upon a peer-to-peer DHT-based overlay, which will orchestrate a large number of clients and devices at geo-distributed sites or servers. DHT-based overlay had been widely used in various kinds of systems for file storage, state recovery, and stream processing [7,8,13,14]. FedPod builds many resource management trees to organize all functionalities. The resource management tree is an aggregation and multicast tree leveraging Scribe [3]. Among the resource management tree, it implements the following functional components: client manager, device monitor, client selector, and communicator. The client resource manager orchestrates the physical computation resources (e.g., CPU, GPU, memory) by aggregating the real-time performance from all clients in the tree. The device monitor traces the runtime status of devices such as servers at a large scale. The client selector makes decisions for choosing a proper set of available clients for new data applications. The communicator handles the messages and communications among all clients in the tree. More details will be introduced later.

When users submit new data applications with models and their configurations to FedPod, the requirements are first sent to the resource management tree. The root node in the resource management tree then analyzes the configurations and estimates the desired resources for the tasks. Then the resource management tree will provide a set of clients with sufficient available computation resources to support such a task. The decision-making will be completed in a short period of time guaranteeing the runtime requirements of users.

2.2 Architecture of Resource Management Trees

The resource management tree is a DHT-based hierarchical tree that leverages Scribe [3] and proximity-aware Pastry overlay [10], which can efficiently organize the huge amount of clients at runtime. FedPod creates many trees in the system in order to dynamically handle applications with various requirements and configurations. Each resource management tree supports application-level group communication and maintains a spanning tree consisting of the clients. The resource tree allows clients flexibly join and leave the tree, so its size can vary from hundreds to millions. By following Scribe [3], the resource management tree uses a pseudorandom key to name a tree, called treeId. Normally, the treeId is the hash of the tree's textual name concatenated with its application's name. Clients can route JOIN messages toward the treeId and messages will reach a client in the tree. The tree can easily support a large number of clients with dynamic memberships by following the routing policy in Scribe.

The resource management tree has the following functional components: client resource manager, client selector, device monitor, and communicator. The client resource manager can organize the real-time resource usage of the following clients in the tree by aggregating the runtime performance of each client. Clients will periodically send the details of resource usage to their upper clients in the tree, and such information will be routed again and again in the tree until reaches the root of the tree. The aggregation of resource usage information can be completed in $O(logN)$ depth, therefore, the root client in the tree can instantly gather the runtime performance of each client. Similarly, the device status including errors or failures can also be immediately acquired by the root client, so as to support the efficient management of device resources.

Further, the resource management tree holds the communicator to collaboratively work with other trees in supporting large-scale applications and scalability. The root client in each resource management tree can share the information of available clients with other trees if that tree cannot find a proper set of clients for future applications. For example, different resource management trees can be across many geo-distributed sites or servers. When one tree has been closely fully booked for several applications, however, it needs to handle more tasks without available clients, the root client can inquire about the nearby trees by sending its needs to other trees via communicator. Other trees can quickly provide their available clients to the querying tree, and these available clients can easily join the querying tree by routing a message. Such a process can be instantly fulfilled in the overlay without incurring long latency.

2.3 Selection of Available Clients

In this subsection, we introduce how to select the proper set of available clients for the specific FL task. It consists of two phases: first, the resource management trees will estimate the overhead of new tasks; second, it utilizes a best-fit based algorithm to find a proper set of available clients for the new tasks. We next elaborate on the details of these two phases.

Estimate the Overhead of New Task. We focus on the overall task completion time T_c of the federated learning application, where the execution processing consists of k iterations. Normally, each iteration of federated learning task includes the model training time T_t and global parameter synchronization time T_s. Therefore, $T_c = \sum_{i=1}^{k}(T_c(i) + T_s(i)) + T_{ini}$, here T_{ini} denotes the initial time of the model and task. The runtime overhead of a federated learning task mainly depends on the size of the dataset, hyper-parameters, and the aggregation of local models. To estimate the overhead of $T_c(i)$ and $T_s(i)$, FedPod collects the configurations and hyper-parameters of the model and requirements from users, such as N_{batch}, $batch_{size}$, N_{gpus}, number of requested clients/instances, etc. It uses the Random Forest algorithm to complete the regression task of estimating overheads by several discrete parameters. It takes input features (e.g., N_{batch}, $batch_{size}$, N_{gpus}, $N_{clients}$, N_{local}), and outputs a vector for estimated resources, which include the requested GPU resource usage N_{gpus}, network communication bandwidth net_{band}, CPU resource usage N_{cpus}, GPU memory usage gpu_{memory}, and estimated aggregation overhead $T_{aggregation}$, etc. In future work, we plan to adopt advanced machine learning models to avoid overfitting and support higher data dimensions.

Best-Fit Based Clients Selection. In a huge cluster of computation nodes, submitting the FL tasks one to one to the cluster of nodes can be extremely time-consuming due to the bottleneck of bandwidth. FedPod adopts the best-fit based client selection so as to efficiently distributed tasks to the cluster and efficiently utilize the resource of each node. We define a performance score S by evaluating different selection of clients based on the features of tasks and clusters. Following prior work by Lai et al. [9], we define the statistical utility of a device i as $utility_{(i)} = \sum_{r=1}^{k}|D_i|\sqrt{\frac{1}{|D_i|}\sum_{d\in|D_i|}loss_{k-1}(d)^2}$, where k denotes the kth iteration of training processing, D_i is the local training data set, and $loss_{k-1}(d)$ is the training loss of the global model from the previous training epoch on sample d. Therefore, the purpose of clients selection to achieve $\min_{\rho\in p_i} S_\rho$, $S_\rho = (1-\lambda)\sum utility_{(i)} + \lambda cost(i)$ where ρ denotes the set id of selected nodes and $\rho \in p_i$ denotes all optional sets of selected nodes, $cost(i)$ denotes the resource usage of the task that mainly refers to the usage of GPU, CPU, and memory, and $\lambda \in (0,1)$ determines the priority of these two factors.

The main idea is to select the set of most suitable clients for the federated learning tasks. FedPod adopts the following steps in choosing the clients: (1) root node in the resource management tree first computes the estimated overhead of the specific task, then it selects the available set of nodes that fulfill the requirements of resources. (2) Calculate the score of the node by assuming allocating the sub-task on the candidate node. (3) Choose the candidate node with the minimal score, and iterate previous steps until no need for more clients.

2.4   Real-Time Resource Management

Resource management trees can collect real-time resource usage from all following clients. This procedure is completed through the aggregation trees. Each client in the tree maintains its routing table that supports the message routing and aggregation in the tree. The real-time resource usage is organized as tuples with the type of resource and its usage, such as $\langle CPU, percentage, size \rangle$, $\langle memory, capacity \rangle$. When routing a message towards a key (usually the treeId), a client forwards its resource usage information to the next client in its routing table with the longest prefix in common with treeId. In the tree with N clients, it is guaranteed that messages can be routed to the appropriate treeId within $O(logN)$ steps.

To avoid the side efforts of failures or stragglers, FedPod maintains leaf sets that can efficiently handle client failures. Each client has its own leaf set, of which half is larger and another half are smaller than the present id. Neighboring clients in its leaf set periodically exchange keep-alive messages. If one client is not responsive for a specific time limit, it will be presumed as failed. Other clients will be notified and use their leaf set to find another proper client. When the failed client recovers, it will notify all clients in its leaf set and other clients will update the information of their leaf set. This procedure can be completed in a very short period of time so that failures will not cause disaster effects in the aggregation of resource usage and client selection.

3   Evaluations

The evaluation experiment is conducted on a testbed of 6 Amazon EC2 instances running Linux Ubuntu 18.04. All instances are Amazon EC2 g4dn.xlarge instances, with each has 4 cores of vCPUs, 16 GB memory, 1 NVIDIA T4 GPU with 16 GB GPU memory, and 200 GB storage. Besides, all instances have a maximum of 10 Gbps network bandwidth. We use Oort [9] as the federated learning processing baseline. For the Oort simulation, one instance will host as the parameter server and the others will be used as workers.

We first evaluate the performance of selecting the proper set of clients and the collection of real-time resource usage information. Figure 2a shows the comparison of the allocation time for selecting proper clients and allocating jobs to clients. FedPod achieves around 15.6%–48.2% less time than Oort. The main reason for reducing the allocation time is that Oort needs to sequentially allocate each task until all workers return their interim weights, which involves heavy network communication and waiting time. Whereas FedPod can parallelly allocate all tasks after collecting the resource usage of all clients. Figure 2b shows the latency of collecting the real-time resource usage information from all clients. Results show that even with a large number of jobs and a huge amount of clients in the system, FedPod can quickly collect the resource usage information to its root clients in the tree. This aggregation process can be completed in $O(logN)$ steps in the Scribe tree, which saves a lot of time for further client selection.

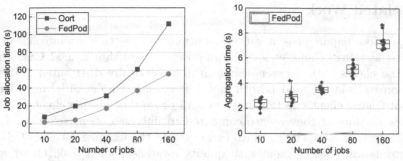

(a) Time of allocating jobs in the cluster.

(b) Time of aggregating resource usage information.

Fig. 2. (a) shows the time for allocating different number of jobs in the cluster. (b) shows the aggregation time of collecting the resource usage details from clients.

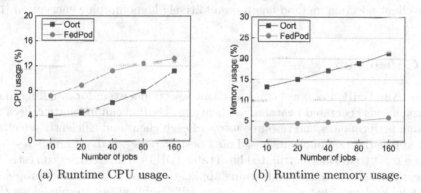

(a) Runtime CPU usage.

(b) Runtime memory usage.

Fig. 3. Runtime performance. (a) shows the CPU usage at runtime. (b) shows the memory usage at runtime.

We next evaluate the runtime overhead. Figure 3a shows the runtime CPU usage comparison of Oort and FedPod. FedPod has a 16.8%–26.4% higher CPU usage than Oort. This is because FedPod maximally utilizes available CPU resources for calculating the utility score and making quick decisions for the clients. Whereas, Oort processes worker feedback as a FIFO, so when there are not many workers, CPU usage is intermittent. If the number of workers increases, Oort's CPU usage may increase significantly, especially if there are multiple workers in the queue of FIFO. Figure 3b shows the runtime memory usage comparison. The memory usage of Oort is almost 2–4 times than FedPod. The main reason for the high memory usage of Oort is the need to cache model and utility information in memory. However, FedPod does not need to cache the model in the memory.

4   Related Work

Many previous papers present various solutions for selecting available clients in federated learning. Zhang et al. [17] propose an algorithm named CSFedAvg, where the clients with a lower degree of non-identically distributed data will be chosen to train the models with higher frequency. Cho et al [5] introduce a Power-of-Choice client selection strategy and prove that biasing client selection increases the rate of convergence compared to unbiased client selection. Deng et al. [6] propose AUCTION, which can evaluate the learning quality of clients and automatically select them with quality awareness for a task. Other work also explores the client selection from different perspectives, such as focusing on the trade-off between maximizing selected clients and minimizing the total energy consumption [15], exploring the correlations between clients to alleviate the accuracy degradation caused by data heterogeneity [12], measuring how a selected subset of clients can represent the whole model [1], or adopting a pluggable client selection method based on additively homomorphic encryption [16], etc.

5   Conclusion

We propose FedPod, a novel efficient client selection system for handling many heterogeneous Federated Learning applications. FedPod can instantly collect the runtime performances and resource usage of each client and efficiently select the most appropriate set of clients based on a best-fit policy. FedPod builds resource management trees via a distributed hash table (DHT). The tree root can estimate the workload of new federated learning applications and find the most proper set of available clients that can handle the specific application. Results show that FedPod can quickly collect the runtime performance of clients and instantly find the proper set of available clients even with a large number of different jobs.

In the future, we will expand the functional components, add more designs to the estimation of runtime overhead, support cross-platform task communication, and ensure good reliability for scalable processing. Additionally, we plan to explore more features to support many other types of distributed deep learning models.

References

1. Balakrishnan, R., Li, T., Zhou, T., Himayat, N., Smith, V., Bilmes, J.: Diverse client selection for federated learning: submodularity and convergence analysis. In: ICML 2021 International Workshop on Federated Learning for User Privacy and Data Confidentiality (2021)
2. Bonawitz, K., et al.: Towards federated learning at scale: system design. Proc. Mach. Learn. Syst. 1, 374–388 (2019)
3. Castro, M., Druschel, P., Kermarrec, A.M., Rowstron, A.I.: Scribe: a large-scale and decentralized application-level multicast infrastructure. IEEE J. Sel. Areas Commun. 20(8), 1489–1499 (2002)

4. Cho, Y.J., Wang, J., Joshi, G.: Client selection in federated learning: convergence analysis and power-of-choice selection strategies. arXiv preprint arXiv:2010.01243 (2020)
5. Cho, Y.J., Wang, J., Joshi, G.: Towards understanding biased client selection in federated learning. In: International Conference on Artificial Intelligence and Statistics, pp. 10351–10375. PMLR (2022)
6. Deng, Y., et al.: Auction: automated and quality-aware client selection framework for efficient federated learning. IEEE Trans. Parallel Distrib. Syst. **33**(8), 1996–2009 (2021)
7. Graffi, K., Masinde, N.: Libresocial: a peer-to-peer framework for online social networks. Concurrency Comput.: Pract. Exp. **33**(8), e6150 (2021)
8. Hassanzadeh-Nazarabadi, Y., Taheri-Boshrooyeh, S., Otoum, S., Ucar, S., Özkasap, Ö.: Dht-based communications survey: architectures and use cases. arXiv preprint arXiv:2109.10787 (2021)
9. Lai, F., Zhu, X., Madhyastha, H.V., Chowdhury, M.: Oort: efficient federated learning via guided participant selection. In: 15th {USENIX} Symposium on Operating Systems Design and Implementation ({OSDI} 21), pp. 19–35 (2021)
10. Rowstron, A., Druschel, P.: Pastry: scalable, decentralized object location, and routing for large-scale peer-to-peer systems. In: Guerraoui, R. (ed.) Middleware 2001. LNCS, vol. 2218, pp. 329–350. Springer, Heidelberg (2001) https://doi.org/10.1007/3-540-45518-3_18
11. Sha, J., Basara, N., Freedman, J., Xu, H.: Flor: a federated learning-based music recommendation engine. In: 2022 International Conference on Computer Communications and Networks (ICCCN) (2022)
12. Tang, M., Ning, X., Wang, Y., Wang, Y., Chen, Y.: Fedgp: correlation-based active client selection for heterogeneous federated learning. arXiv preprint arXiv:2103.13822 (2021)
13. Xu, H., et al.: Oases: an online scalable spam detection system for social networks. In: 2018 IEEE 11th International Conference on Cloud Computing (CLOUD), pp. 98–105. IEEE (2018)
14. Xu, H., Liu, P., Cruz-Diaz, S., Silva, D.D., Hu, L.: Sr3: customizable recovery for stateful stream processing systems. In: Proceedings of the 21st International Middleware Conference (Middleware), pp. 251–264 (2020)
15. Yu, L., Albelaihi, R., Sun, X., Ansari, N., Devetsikiotis, M.: Jointly optimizing client selection and resource management in wireless federated learning for internet of things. IEEE Internet Things J. **9**(6), 4385–4395 (2021)
16. Zhang, S., Li, Z., Chen, Q., Zheng, W., Leng, J., Guo, M.: Dubhe: towards data unbiasedness with homomorphic encryption in federated learning client selection. In: 50th International Conference on Parallel Processing, pp. 1–10 (2021)
17. Zhang, W., Wang, X., Zhou, P., Wu, W., Zhang, X.: Client selection for federated learning with non-iid data in mobile edge computing. IEEE Access **9**, 24462–24474 (2021)

Hestia: A Cost-Effective Multi-dimensional Resource Utilization for Microservices Execution in the Cloud

Jiahua Huang[1,2], Kenneth B. Kent[3], Jerome Yen[4], and Yang Wang[1,2(✉)]

[1] Shenzhen Institutes of Advanced Technology, Chinese Academy of Sciences,
Shenzhen, China
yang.wang1@siat.ac.cn
[2] University of Chinese Academy of Sciences, Beijing, China
[3] University of New Brunswick Frederiction, Fredericton, Canada
[4] University of Macau, Macau, China

Abstract. It is well-known that effective resource utilization is a critical factor in providing high quality microservicess in cloud computing. In a large-scale cluster, if each machine can save a small amount of resources, a huge effect could be made to significantly reduce the overall computing cost as the saved resources across the cluster can be gathered into a large resource pool to facilitate the computation as a whole. As such, how to effectively allocate the resources in a single host is critical to the success of this saving strategy. To this end, we propose a multi-dimensional resource allocation algorithm, called *Hestia*, for a single machine in a stand-alone environment with each dimension having limited resources. The algorithm is designed by leveraging dynamic programming (DP) techniques to squeeze the occupied resources of the existing microservices without compromising their performance, and leave the saved resources for other newly deployed microservices. Our experimental results show that compared with the default case, this method can save up to 15% of the resources for a single machine while ensuring the stability of online microservices.

Keywords: Resource allocation · Dynamic programming · Single-machine

1 Introduction

The large-scale implementation of cloud computing makes microservices applications increasingly portable. They also make the deployment, upgrade, rollback, and expansion of microservices more efficient. The application of container choreography, based on Kubernetes, automates most processes without manual participation. However, today's container choreography applications schedule services and tasks in the overall cluster dimension. There is no perfect system for resource allocation and services scheduling of a single machine dimension. Each time a user, who does not know how many resources are left on their machine, apply for a certain amount of resource quota for their applications, based on their experience, the scheduling system will schedule the applications to appropriate machines according to the quota and some restrictions. When services needs to be upgraded or taken down, the scheduling system kills the application and reclaims resources to the resource pool. However, in day-to-day situations, application developers leave a certain amount of cache for resources, and request more resources than they need when requesting resources. A large number of online services use only a small portion of the requested resources most of the time. From the data published by Baidu, the daily CPU utilization in their clusters is around 15%. This results in wasted resources on a single machine. If we can properly recover some resources for other applications when the load is relatively low and return them when the load is high, this will greatly improve the efficiency of using resources on the whole machine and also ensure the stability of online services.

Most of the previous studies were focused on jobs, and resources were allocated so that a series of jobs could be completed in the shortest time, or the most jobs could be completed in the acceptable time. It is very difficult to provide appropriate resources for a job. Previously, many researchers optimized the job scheduling algorithm through a large number of experiments to reduce the execution time and cost of the overall job set [6,8–10,18]. However, the characteristics of application services and jobs are different. Assignments can be paused or restarted for a short time. The application services must always be healthy to receive requests from clients. The task is measured by the length of time it takes. Application services use access latency indicating health. When the access latency is high or there is no return value, the application services resources are insufficient. Therefore, the resource scheduling of application services has different emphases from that of jobs, and the scheduling algorithm needs to evolve under new conditions.

A few researchers focus on the balance between resource utilization and quality-of-services guarantees of microservices in cloud computing scenarios. The multi-dimensional queue load optimization algorithm is used to dynamically select requests from classes and improve the utilization of virtual machines through effective and fair load balancing. Then the load balancing algorithm is implemented to avoid the under-utilization and over-utilization of resources and improve the delay time of each type of request [12]. Emeakaroha et al. proposed a new scheduling heuristic that considers multiple SLA parameters [5]. Pradhan and et al. proposed an improved round-robin resource allocation algorithm to meet customer demand by reducing waiting time [11]. Zhou et al. designed and implemented a load balancing scheme based on a dynamic resource allocation policy, which monitors in real time the VM and PM resource utilization, including CPU, memory and network, and then performs instant resource reallocation for virtual machines (VMs) running on the same PM to achieve local VM load balancing [19].

However, when online services are at low load, it is still a challenge to allocate a number of resources, which maintains a minimum acceptable level, to recover some of the wasted resources that have been allocated but not used. This paper proposes a dynamic programming-based services resource scheduling algorithm that guarantees optimal resource allocation scheduling for multiple services in a single machine dimension.

The services resource allocation process on a single machine is very similar to the dynamic selection process of dynamic programming. Decisions need to be made when selecting the appropriate resource quota for each services. Because the total resources are fixed, the resource quota decision of each services will affect the resource quota decision of other services. Therefore, the selection of decisions at each stage cannot be arbitrarily determined. It depends on the current state of affairs that affects future development. When the decisions at each stage are determined, a decision sequence is formed. Therefore we choose to use dynamic programming to complete the calculation of the final resource allocation quota for each services.

Through experimentation, the services quality of different services under different resources and load environments is obtained first. Different resource allocation combinations are equivalent to different states in the dynamic planning process. Through these prior data, the resource allocation is adjusted regularly in the stand-alone dimension, the algorithm completes the decision of each state, and calculates the resources of all services at this time. It is guaranteed that the services obtains the least amount of resources under the condition of guaranteeing stability over a period.

When the entire environment is under low load, resources can be effectively saved by using sub-algorithms to schedule and allocate resources. At the same time, when the application load rises, the stability of the online services is ensured by returning resources. We have built two clusters with different hardware environments and selected the more common online applications on the market today as examples. We have implemented and verified the overall implementation of the algorithm on each of the two clusters and obtained the result that using the Hestia algorithm can save up to 15% of resources on the machine.

The organization of the paper is as follows: We introduce some related work regarding the order dispatching in Sect. 2, and then describe the formulation and notation of the order dispatching problem in Sect. 3 and build a distributed multi-queue model with the proposed algorithm in Sect. 4 and Sect. 5. We present the simulation studies to validate our methods in Sect. 6 and Sect. 7, followed by the conclusion in the last section.

2   Related Work

In this section we will discuss some of the work related to services resource scheduling.

In today's cloud computing scenario, the infrastructure level allows different services to share certain resources to maximize resource utilization. At the same time, how to efficiently use limited resources to complete the most tasks has become an important problem in the field of cloud computing. An efficient resource scheduling algorithm can prevent many resources from being idle, which can be used to deploy more services and complete more functions.

Assi et al. address the Scalable Traffic Management (STM) problem in the cloud using a new decomposition method [1]. With the help of STM, the maximum link load can be reduced, thus ensuring load balancing among users in the network. Another work by Babu et al. took a deep dive into task scheduling in cloud environments using bee behavior [7]. Bee behavior was used to obtain optimal machine utilization by leveraging the foraging behavior of bees to effectively balance the load of virtual machines in a cloud environment. To improve resource performance, Singh and Bawa [14] studied a task scheduling heuristic algorithm, which optimized two important criteria to improve the performance of resources i.e., makespan time and resource utilization. Stavrinides et al. [15] introduced EDF, HLF and LSTF algorithms to schedule multiple tasks in a uniformly distributed real-time system. The main goal of the algorithm is to obtain high-quality (precise) results and provide guarantees for all jobs that reach the system. Singh et al. [13] proposed an agent-based load balancing algorithm and provided dynamic load balancing for cloud environments with the help of an autonomous model. Although load balancing is guaranteed, optimization is not achieved. To overcome this problem, [16], a budget-driven scheduling algorithm is designed using Global Greedy Budget (GGB) and Gradual Refinement (GR) to guarantee performance optimization. Beaumont et al. [2] adopted a greedy heuristic method to discuss the problem of resource allocation in a heterogeneous manner under the premise of guaranteeing throughput and cost. Cloud resource scheduling based on improved particle swarm optimization was proposed by Wang et al. [17]. According to the characteristics that cloud computing resources are subject to user time and budget requirements, a resource scheduling model based on a particle swarm optimization algorithm is designed.

Most of the previous work is to optimize the resource scheduling of the overall dimension of the cluster, and there are few works to manage and schedule the resources of the single-machine dimension. The algorithm proposed in this paper is based on dynamic programming to calculate the most appropriate resource quota for each services on a single machine, to save some resources from each machine to achieve the purpose of optimizing the overall cluster resource allocation.

3   Problems and Challenges

Compared with traditional distributed computing and parallel computing, the resource pool of cloud computing is generally composed of special resources. The server is pre-composed, and cloud computing is oriented to many types of users. Therefore, some traditional resource scheduling and management techniques are not applicable in the cloud computing environment. At the same time, the characteristics of tasks running in the cloud computing environment are different, and the physical environment of a single machine will also be slightly different, such as CPU frequency, network bandwidth, and cache size. Therefore, it is necessary to use a variety of different resource scheduling strategies to achieve maximum efficiency.

In a cloud computing scenario, there will be several applications running on a single machine. With a limited amount of resources, if we can make the applications carry more traffic we can improve the efficiency of the utilization of the single machine's resources. How to allocate the limited resources becomes the most important issue. Some tasks have high CPU requirements, such as function tasks, and some tasks have high GPU requirements, such as reasoning tasks. Each task has its own unique requirements for various heterogeneous resources, so it is a critical issue to ensure those resources are used in the right place by compressing the resources of certain applications and allocating them to other applications while maintaining quality of services.

In order to solve the above problems, we face several challenges:

- How to know if the resources allocated to an application are insufficient or overflowing.
- How to design the resource reallocation algorithm (how many resources are appropriate for each application).
- Whether the allocated resources will vary from machine to machine depending on the architecture.

Faced with the above problems, this paper proposes a resource allocation algorithm based on dynamic programming in a stand-alone environment.

4 Framework

This section introduces the overall framework of the Hestia algorithm deployment environment and its position in the resource scheduling algorithm of the entire cluster.

In order to solve the problem presented in the previous section, we design and implement a system that is divided into three main modules, namely the test module, the calculation module and the scheduling module. In the test module, we will test the capacity of services for different resource limits, and calculate the stability of services provided by various services under a number of configured resource limits. The calculation module of resource quota will combine the data from the test module with the Hestia algorithm to calculate the allocated amount of resources required for each service. The scheduling module will then allocate the data calculated by the quota calculation module to specific nodes and reallocate resources to different services, and redeploy the services after adjusting the resources. The specific architecture diagram is shown in Fig. 1.

Our proposed Hestia algorithm is implemented in the calculation module of the resource quota, where we calculate the most appropriate resource quota for each services based on the data obtained from the test module as an input.

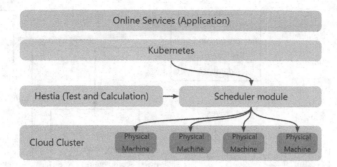

Fig. 1. Overall framework

5   Hestia Algorithm

In real life, there is a kind of activity process, which because of its particularity, can be divided into a number of interrelated stages, each of which needs to make decisions, so that the whole process achieves the best activity offect. Therefore, the selection of decisions at each stage cannot be arbitrarily determined. It depends on the current situation and affects the future development. When the decision of each stage is determined, a decision sequence is formed, and thus an activity route of the whole process is determined. This kind of problem is regarded as a multi-stage process with a chain structure. In the multistage decision problem, the decisions taken by stages are generally associated with the time, the decision depends on the current state, and then causes the transfer of state, a decision sequence is produced in a state of change, it is the meaning of "dynamic", says the solution process of multi-stage decision optimization for dynamic planning method [3]. Figure 2 shows the timing and conditions of Hestia's actual operation on a single machine.

5.1   Algorithm Details

From the previous preparations, we have obtained the services quality performance of all services under different resource and load combinations. The functions of application services are different, and the sensitivity to resources and load is also different. Some services only require a small amount of resources to run stably. As the load of some services increases, in order to meet the stability of the services, the resources required by the services will also increase. Because the total amount of resources is limited, each resource allocation will affect the total amount of the next resource allocation, so it is very suitable to use dynamic programming to solve this problem. Algorithm 1 is the overall flow of our proposed dynamic programming algorithm.

We have five input values, which are the upper limit of the number of CPU cores of the machine, the online memory capacity, the names of all services, the online load, and the quality of services of each services under different resource

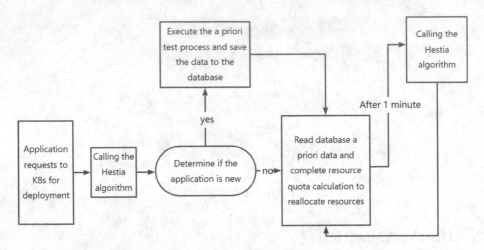

Fig. 2. Hestia executes the process in the real environment

quotas. The last input value QoS has been calculated in the previous preparation. The algorithm can finally determine a resulting distribution matrix. The values in the matrix represent how the S microservices can be combined to achieve the best quality of all microservices when the resource upper limit is CPU, mem, and L. First, initialize the case where S is 1, as follows:

$$result(S_1, CPU, mem, L) = \frac{f_S(CPU, mem, L)}{f_S(CPU_{total}, mem_{total}, L)} \tag{1}$$

This value represents the ratio of the quality of services that can obtain all resources of a single machine under limited resource conditions, and we call it the relative value of quality of services. The purpose of not directly using the quality of services as a basis is to avoid differences in the quantitative set of services quality of different services, so that there will be no obvious difference in the changes of some small microservices in front of large microservices. The final value obtained by the algorithm is the sum of the relative values of services quality after each services obtains the optimal resource allocation ratio when the resource has an upper limit. To obtain the final resource allocation quota for each services, it is necessary to further decompose the results.

As shown in Algorithm 2, we traverse from the last allocated services to get the maximum value of the relative value of the total quality of services. We obtain the resource allocation value of the last allocated services at this time, then subtract the resources allocated by this services from the upper limit of resources, and then enter the penultimate services allocated resources. In this way, the amount of resources allocated to each services can be obtained.

The entire algorithm will run in this way every 2 min to prevent the traffic from skyrocketing at certain times, resulting in insufficient allocation of online microservices resources and a serious decline in services quality. Dynamically running this algorithm ensures that at each time interval services can have an

---

Algorithm 1: Algorithm for Resource Calculation

Input: input parameters CPU_{total}, mem_{total}, $services$, L_{total}, f_S
Output: output result(S,CPU_{total},mem_{total},L_{total})

1 **for** S_n *in range services* **do**
2   **for** $CPU \leq CPU_{total}$ **do**
3   **for** $mem \leq mem_{total}$ **do**
4   **for** $L \leq L_{total}$ **do**
5   result(S_n,CPU,mem,L) $\leftarrow$ result(S_{n-1},CPU_{total}−CPU, mem_{total}−mem,L_{total}−L) $*(n-1)/n + f_S$(CPU,mem,L)$/n * f_S$(CPU_{total},mem_{total},L)
6   **end**
7   **end**
8   **end**
9 **end**

Algorithm 2: Algorithm for Resource Allocation

Input: input parameters result(S,CPU_{total},mem_{total},L_{total}),L
Output: output Allocation(S)

1 **for** S *in range services[..-1]* **do**
2   QoS_S,CPU_S,mem_S $\leftarrow$ min result(S,CPU< CPU_{total},mem< mem_{total},L)
   $CPU_{total} \leftarrow CPU_{total} - CPU_S$ $mem_{total} \leftarrow mem_{total} - mem_S$
3 **end**

---

appropriate resource quota. It does not waste resources, and also ensures the stability of the services. At the same time, the algorithm executes when a new services is deployed on the machine. After that, starting with the new services deployment time, resource allocation is re-allocated every 30 min.

6 Implementation

In this section, we discuss the design of the verification of the Hestia algorithm. To be able to demonstrate the validity of the Hestia algorithm, we built a small cluster of three machines, all configured as shown in Table 1, called master, child node 1 and child node 2. We used Kubernetes to manage the services on the three machines, and we pulled the latest versions of the five application images from Sect. 5.1 and deployed them via deployment with a pod on child node 1. At the same time, on child node 2, we pulled images of each of the five applications in turn and tested them for QoS on all resource ratios. The test results were stored in the deployed database in the master node. The overall architecture is shown in the Fig. 1, with the same machines used in child node 1 and child node 2 to ensure that the test results in child node 2 can be used in child node 1.

We deployed all our services on either child node 1 or child node 2. All the services were deployed on the same machine and each service was followed by a specific container to host the requests received by the services. In addition, we

Table 1. Computer hardware information

Hardware	Information
CPU	Intel Core i9-10900K 3.70 GHz
Memory	Corsair DDR4 3000 Mhz 16 GB * 4
Graphics card	Nvidia GeForce RTX 3080
SSD	Samsung SSD 970 EVO 500 GB
HHD	Seagate ST2000DM005-2CW102 2 TB

deployed a traffic sender, specifically a Java web application that can send the uploaded request parameters to a specified location with specific requirements (speed, asynchronous/synchronous, latency cap, etc.), and can monitor the whole process in real time to collect specific information about the experimental process (including whether the request is in error, whether the request returns a timeout, or the QPS, etc.).

6.1 Preparation

In this section we will discuss the preparation of the resource scheduling algorithm.

The resource scheduling algorithm of dynamic planning is based on the quality of service of each service under different resource quotas and loads. So at the beginning of the experiment, we combine all possible resource quotas and test the quality of service for each service under these combination conditions. This paper chooses five representative services to complete this experiment, namely MySQL, Memcached, Xapiand, Nginx and MongoDB [4].

We tested each resource quota for each service more than 10 times. We ranked the quality of service from lowest to highest and recorded the average value of the 10 points data closest to the middle as the service quality of the final service under this resource limit. It follows that

$$f_S(R_1, R_2, ..., L) = QoS_S = T_{requests} \tag{2}$$

S represents a service, R represents the amount of a resource, and L represents the load. In each of these combinations, we can get the QoS of this services. In this experiment, only CPU and memory resources are selected for resource allocation, and L is quantified by throughput. There are many other resources as shown in Fig. 3, which can also be used in the algorithm.

Resource Isolation. We use Kubernetes to manage the whole system and deploy all services on Kubernetes as pods. The reason for using Kubernetes is that it can easily complete resource isolation through a Cgroup, which provides a good guarantee for our experiment.

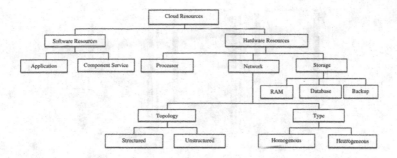

Fig. 3. Some other resources.

Load. We kept the load on the services by randomly sending requests from other servers to the test machine. The value of the load is quantified as throughput. The types of requests are random to ensure fairness. To avoid the impact of network delay, all requests are on the same LAN.

Quality of Services. The quality of services for each service is measured by the time it takes to complete all requests. Another server was used to send all consecutive requests to the tested services. We will eventually calculate the time between sending the first request and completing all requests.

6.2 Detail

First we need to test the QoS values for all applications in child node 2 for different resource ratios, i.e. the time taken to complete all requests. We will test all applications in turn, each with its own set of test traffic.

These test traffic sets are stored on the master node, and at the start of each test, a client is started on the master node to read out the traffic from this application's corresponding traffic set and send it to the test application in child node 2. At the same time, this client also calculates the traffic completion time. If the failure rate of the test traffic reaches 10% or more, we consider this resource ratio too small to guarantee the services stability of this application, and the maximum resource allocated for the test is one third of the machine's maximum allocable resources, i.e. when the machine has 24 cores, each application gets a maximum of 8 cores. Each application will be tested 3 times for each resource ratio, and the results will be averaged over the 3 times.

Eventually we will get a QoS value for the application with different resource ratios; the smaller this value is, the better the quality of services. When the test traffic failure rate is too high, the test will be deemed to have failed and the QoS will then be set to 1,000,000.

Eventually when all five applications are deployed, we will calculate the sum of the maximum QPS that the five applications can handle. At the same time, the applications are deployed in the same order with an even distribution of resources, and the sum of the maximum QPS that the five applications can

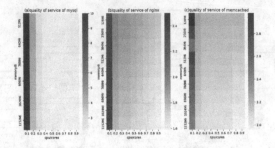

Fig. 4. MySQL, Nginx and Memcached's quality of services, the color represents the time it took to complete all requests.

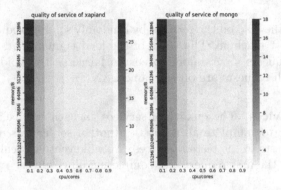

Fig. 5. Mongo and Xapiand's quality of services, the color represents the time to complete all requests.

withstand in this case, is calculated and compared to the results using the Hestia algorithm.

7   Evaluation

In this section, we discuss the performance of the algorithm in actual experiments. First of all, we tested the service quality of each service under different resource combinations.

Figure 4(a) shows MySQL's quality of service. Since the services cannot start with less than 512 MB of memory, the display starts with 512 MB. It can be seen that MySQL does not improve the quality of service significantly under this load when the CPU resource is greater than 0.4 cores. So the most appropriate resource combination for MySQL services under this load is (CPU = 0.4 cores, memory = 512 MB).

As shown in Fig. 4(b) and (c), the quality of services for Nginx and Memcached tends to change with resources in relatively the same way, requiring only a small amount of resources to run the services steadily.

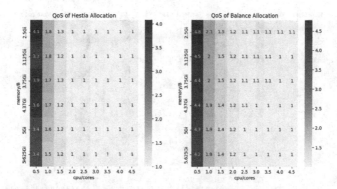

Fig. 6. The comparison between the average allocation of resources and the relative value of services quality allocated by Hestia algorithm.

As shown in Fig. 5, Mongo and Xapiand are much more resource sensitive than the other three services. When there are few resources, the quality of service is relatively poor, but as the resources increase, when the CPU gets 0.5 cores or more, the quality of service will tend to be stable.

We first deploy five services sequentially on the machine, and then use two methods to test the Hestia algorithm. In the first method, we apply for the maximum resource quota (2 CPU cores and 5 GB memory) for each service at one time, and then deploy five services at the same time under the same load. The second method is that each service deployment is separated by 15 min, because the Hestia algorithm will be executed again after each completion of 10 min. These two methods are then compared with the Hestia algorithm without invocation. Machines that do not invoke the Hestia algorithm will use the method of equal allocation of resources. Because MySQL needs more resources, it will allocate slightly more resources to MySQL as appropriate to ensure that it can run and provide services normally.

Through our large-scale experiments, we found that the values assigned by the above two methods are basically the same, and the relative values of services quality obtained are basically the same. As shown in Fig. 6, compared with the even distribution of resources, the relative value of service quality using the Hestia algorithm will decrease by 10% to 20% when the resources are small, indicating that the Hestia algorithm allocates the limited resources on a single machine more reasonably. The resources of some services are reduced when the services quality improvement is close to the bottleneck, and this part of the resources is allocated to the rest of the newly deployed tasks, so that the entire machine can deploy more tasks and provide more functions.

Next, we repeated other loads several times, doubling and tripling the previous load. The three experimental results are shown in Fig. 7.

We can see that as the load increases, the relative value of services quality will increase when the resources are fewer which means that more resources are

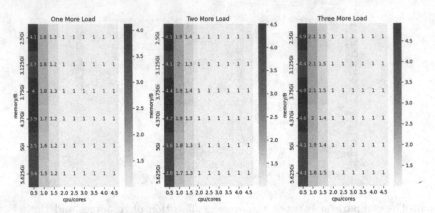

Fig. 7. The relative value of services quality after doubling, doubling and tripling the load when calling the Hestia algorithm.

Table 2. Computer hardware information

Hardware	Information
CPU	Intel Core i5-9400f 2.90 GHz
Memory	ADATA DDR4 2666 Mhz 8 GB * 2
Graphics card	Nvidia GeForce RTX 1660 SUPER
SSD	TOSHIBA SSD RC-500 500 GB

required to obtain the same service quality after the load increases. This is close to our actual theory.

After this, we compared a scheduler using the Hestia scheduling algorithm with a scheduler that did not apply the Hestia scheduling algorithm, using the same model configuration to deploy five applications on the machines in the same random order. A scheduler that did not use Hestia would divide the resources equally among all applications, so we limited the total amount of resources, and then counted the time it took for all applications to complete all requests.

The overall results are shown in Fig. 8. In the meantime, we have replicated all the previous experiments on another platform, with the specific model configuration shown in Table 2. On this platform, although the performance of the platform is somewhat lacking, we obtained roughly consistent trends, as shown in Fig. 9.

Because of the drop in machine performance, the quality of services is correspondingly more affected by the resource limit, as shown in Fig. 9, overall completion time drops in varying degrees compared to the higher performance machines. However, the overall trend is unchanged; with fewer resources, the use of the Hestia algorithm provides a greater degree of stability and takes less time to complete all requests, and as more resources become available, the sensitivity of the application to the amount of resources' decreases, and then the difference

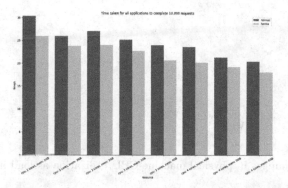

Fig. 8. Total time taken by all applications to complete all requests on a high performance machine.

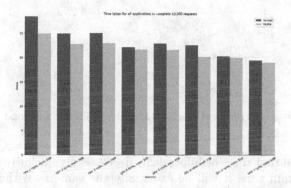

Fig. 9. Total time taken by all applications to complete all requests on a low performance machine.

between the two then becomes smaller, and it may occasionally even happen that using the Hestia algorithm instead takes more time.

As can be seen in Fig. 10, as the traffic load increases over time, the CPU utilization of the experiments with the Hestia algorithm is consistently higher than without it by about 5 to 10%.

At the same time, physical machines using the Hestia algorithm can improve memory utilization by around 10% (Fig. 11). The Hestia algorithm increases the efficiency of both CPU and memory usage while maintaining quality of services.

We also tested the additional consumption caused by the computation of the algorithm preparation phase, which is required once in advance for each type of application, and only when a new application is deployed. The main impact of this process is the scheduling latency of the application from application to deployment, as shown in Table 3.

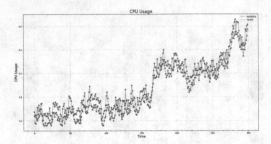

Fig. 10. Changes in physical machine CPU utilization as load increases.

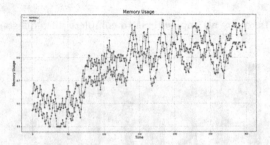

Fig. 11. Changes in physical machine Memory utilization as load increases.

It can be seen that the scheduling delay decreases significantly as time grows, and after a certain time it will be essentially the same as without the Hestia algorithm.

Table 3. Additional consumption caused by Hestia

Type	30 min	60 min	2 h	12 h
Hestia	358 s	74 s	21 s	15 s
No Hestia	12 s	12 s	13 s	12 s

8   Conclusion

This paper presents the Hestia algorithm, a dynamic programming-based algorithm for optimizing the multi-dimensional resource allocation and resource utilization efficiency of microservices on a single machine. The algorithm requires testing the quality of services of microservices under various resource configurations in advance. It can identify some allocated, but inefficient, resources in a microservices with small overall resource usage and reclaim them for allocation to services that need them more. The resource utilisation efficiency of the whole machine is improved to achieve cost reduction and efficiency. In our experiments, we found that using the Hestia algorithm in different resource quotas, the quality of services of the application can be improved by up to 15%.

There is still much room for further improvement in this work, such as determining the factors that define good or bad online service quality, rather than the time to complete the services at a single time. Also, determine whether the different requirements of these different applications for heterogeneous resources have an impact on the results and whether the algorithm is still valid if they are all compute-intensive or access-intensive applications. Whether the overall algorithm can be focused when allocating resources to different types of applications, rather than all applications being measured against one standard. Likewise finding a similar approach to optimizing resource allocation for offline applications or in offline hybrid environments. These are all questions that need to be addressed, and we will continue to dig into this area of information in future work in the hope of obtaining more helpful results.

Acknowledgment. This work was supported in part by Key-Area Research and Development Program of Guangdong Province (2020B010164002) and in part by Chinese Academy of Sciences President's International Fellowship Initiative (2023VTA0001).

References

1. Assi, C., Ayoubi, S., Sebbah, S., Shaban, K.: Towards scalable traffic management in cloud data centers. IEEE Trans. Commun. **62**(3), 1033–1045 (2014)
2. Beaumont, O., Eyraud-Dubois, L., Caro, C.T., Rejeb, H.: Heterogeneous resource allocation under degree constraints. IEEE Trans. Parallel Distrib. Syst. **24**(5), 926–937 (2012)
3. Bellman, R.: Dynamic programming. Science **153**(3731), 34–37 (1966)
4. Chen, S., Delimitrou, C., Martínez, J.F.: Parties: QoS-aware resource partitioning for multiple interactive services. In: Proceedings of the Twenty-Fourth International Conference on Architectural Support for Programming Languages and Operating Systems, ASPLOS 2019, New York, NY, USA, pp. 107–120. Association for Computing Machinery (2019)
5. Emeakaroha, V.C., Brandic, I., Maurer, M., Breskovic, I.: SLA-aware application deployment and resource allocation in clouds. In: 2011 IEEE 35th Annual Computer Software and Applications Conference Workshops, pp. 298–303. IEEE (2011)
6. Hu, J., Gu, J., Sun, G., Zhao, T.: A scheduling strategy on load balancing of virtual machine resources in cloud computing environment. In: 2010 3rd International Symposium on Parallel Architectures, Algorithms and Programming, pp. 89–96. IEEE (2010)
7. LD, D.B., Krishna, P.V.: Honey bee behavior inspired load balancing of tasks in cloud computing environments. Appl. Soft Comput. **13**(5), 2292–2303 (2013)
8. Lee, Y.C., Wang, C., Zomaya, A.Y., Zhou, B.B.: Profit-driven service request scheduling in clouds. In: 2010 10th IEEE/ACM International Conference on Cluster, Cloud and Grid Computing, pp. 15–24 (2010)

9. Liu, K., Jin, H., Chen, J., Liu, X., Yuan, D., Yang, Y.: A compromised-time-cost scheduling algorithm in SwinDeW-C for instance-intensive cost-constrained workflows on a cloud computing platform. Int. J. High Perform. Comput. Appl. **24**(4), 445–456 (2010)
10. Pandey, S., Wu, L., Guru, S.M., Buyya, R.: A particle swarm optimization-based heuristic for scheduling workflow applications in cloud computing environments. In: 2010 24th IEEE International Conference on Advanced Information Networking and Applications, pp. 400–407. IEEE (2010)
11. Pradhan, P., Behera, P.K., Ray, B.: Modified round robin algorithm for resource allocation in cloud computing. Procedia Comput. Sci. **85**, 878–890 (2016)
12. Priya, V., Kumar, C.S., Kannan, R.: Resource scheduling algorithm with load balancing for cloud service provisioning. Appl. Soft Comput. **76**, 416–424 (2019)
13. Singh, A., Juneja, D., Malhotra, M.: Autonomous agent based load balancing algorithm in cloud computing. Procedia Comput. Sci. **45**, 832–841 (2015)
14. Singh, S., Bawa, R.: Optimized assignment of independent task for improving resources performance in computational grid. Int. J. Grid Comput. Appl. (IJGCA) **6** (2015)
15. Stavrinides, G.L., Karatza, H.D.: Scheduling multiple task graphs with end-to-end deadlines in distributed real-time systems utilizing imprecise computations. J. Syst. Softw. **83**(6), 1004–1014 (2010)
16. Wang, Y., Shi, W.: Budget-driven scheduling algorithms for batches of mapreduce jobs in heterogeneous clouds. IEEE Trans. Cloud Comput. **2**(3), 306–319 (2014)
17. Wang, Y., Wang, J., Wang, C., Song, X.: Research on resource scheduling of cloud based on improved particle swarm optimization algorithm. In: Liu, D., Alippi, C., Zhao, D., Hussain, A. (eds.) BICS 2013. LNCS (LNAI), vol. 7888, pp. 118–125. Springer, Heidelberg (2013). https://doi.org/10.1007/978-3-642-38786-9_14
18. Yang, Z., Yin, C., Liu, Y.: A cost-based resource scheduling paradigm in cloud computing. In: 2011 12th International Conference on Parallel and Distributed Computing, Applications and Technologies, pp. 417–422. IEEE (2011)
19. Zhou, W., Yang, S., Fang, J., Niu, X., Song, H.: VMCTune: a load balancing scheme for virtual machine cluster using dynamic resource allocation. In: 2010 Ninth International Conference on Grid and Cloud Computing, pp. 81–86. IEEE (2010)

Optimizing Cache Accesses with Tensor Memory Format Search for Transformers in TVM

Xianghuan He[1,2], Xitong Gao[1(✉)], Juanjuan Zhao[1], Chengxi Gao[1], and Kejiang Ye[1]

[1] Shenzhen Institute of Advanced Technology, Chinese Academy of Sciences, Shenzhen, China
{xh.he,xt.gao,jj.zhao,chengxi.gao,kj.ye}@siat.ac.cn
[2] University of Chinese Academy of Sciences, Beijing, China

Abstract. Transformer-based models have achieved great success in natural language processing and computer vision applications. These models, however, often comprise a large number of parameters. Furthermore, tend to be computationally intensive. This presents a challenge in deploying them on resource-constrained devices. Using deep learning compilers, *e.g.* TVM, to compile these models can reap the performance benefit gained by tailoring CUDA kernels specifically for the target GPU devices. In this paper, we focus on complementing existing compiler optimization passes in TVM by further exploring the impact of tensor memory formats used by intermediate activations on cache accesses and its performance implications. First, building on top of the graph-based abstraction, we express each layer node, *e.g.* multi-layer perceptron (MLP) and self-attention layers, using Einstein summation or Einsum-based notations. Edges formed by intermediate tensors thus connecting layer nodes as their inputs and outputs. As intermediate tensors are typically stored in memory contiguously, their memory formats in terms of the ordering of its dimensions, may exhibit the notable effect on cache access behavior, and strided memory accesses are typically slower than contiguous ones. Yet existing compiler frameworks focus on layer-wise optimizations, and often neglected the impact of tensor memory formats of the layer's inputs and outputs on the performance of the resulting kernels. To this end, this paper proposes to optimize the performance of compiled models by searching for optimal memory formats for all intermediate tensors. We then use the MLP-Mixer model architecture as a case study of the optimization process and deploy the resulting optimized models with TVM on target GPUs. As exhaustive searching requires a substantial computational cost, we thus propose algorithms to efficiently navigate the search space of memory formats of intermediate tensors. Applying the algorithm on an MLP-Mixer model with 42 mixer-layers, we can achieve 23.7% inference performance enhancement.

Keywords: Deep learning · Deep learning compiler · Transformers · TVM · Tensor memory formats

© The Author(s), under exclusive license to Springer Nature Switzerland AG 2022
K. Ye and L.-J. Zhang (Eds.): CLOUD 2022, LNCS 13731, pp. 39–53, 2022.
https://doi.org/10.1007/978-3-031-23498-9_4

1 Introduction

Deep neural networks (DNN) can now achieve remarkable results in many fields of applications, such as image classification, speech recognition, and natural language processing (NLP) [1]. Most of the well-known work in computer vision relies on convolutional neural networks(CNN) [2–4]. In recent years, Transformers [5] have surpassed CNNs in attaining state-of-the-art (SOTA) task accuracies, thanks to the significant breakthroughs made in the field of NLP [6–10], and computer vision [11–14].

In general, transformer-based models use residual blocks, typically composed of two components: a multi-layer perceptron (MLP) layer and a self-attention module. Though such a structure allows the model to focus on more feature information, the cost of implementing a transformer-based model is relatively high. Table 1 lists the number of trained parameters and the number of multiplication and addition (MAdds) operations required to make inference on one image on popular transformer models such as the vision transformer (VIT) [11], data-efficient image transformer (DeiT) [12] and the MLP-Mixer [15]. We can see that compared with the residual-network (ResNet) [2] with a CNN-based structure, although transformer-based models can bring substantial improvement in accuracy, they often require a lot more parameter and consume more computational resources. Following the architectural design of transformers, MLP-Mixer [15] shows that it is possible to achieve SOTA results on image classification tasks, where all trainable layers are MLP layers. However, it is notable that the MLP-based architecture also brings a considerable amount of parameters (59 million) and 44.8 billion Adds operations for accurate inference of an image.

Table 1. Details of Vision Transformer-based model variants.

Model	Model configurations			Accuracy (%)
	Input size	Params (M)	MAdds (B)	
ResNet-152 [2]	224	60	11.3	78.3
ViT-B/16 [11]	384	86	55.4	77.9
ViT-L/16 [11]	384	307	190.7	76.5
DeiT-Ti [12] (ViT+reg)	224	5	1.3	72.2
DeiT-S [12] (ViT+reg)	224	22	4.6	79.8
DeiT-B [12] (ViT+reg)	224	86	1705	81.8
Mixer B/16	224	59	12.7	76.4
Mixer L/16	224	207	44.8	71.8

Targeting the implementation of deep neural network models, today's popular frameworks Pytorch [16], TensorFlow [17] and Caffe [18] all have their respective tool-flows to compile deep learning models into static directed acyclic graphs (DAGs) representing the data flow of computations, and they further optimize these graphs by graph optimization techniques, and carry out inference using pre-compiled kernels. On top of this, deep learning compilers additionally incorporates the specifications of the targeted hardware, and use code generation and optimization techniques well known in the compiler community to specifically tailor compiled implementations of models. Some of the better-known open-source deep learning compiler frameworks include XLA from Google [17], Apache TVM [19], Intel nGraph [20], and Facebook's Tensor Compression (TC) [21].

As pointed out by [22], device memory access often presents a bottleneck for algorithm performance, we need to maximize data reuse in each memory hierarchy to leverage as much as possible the limited bandwidths from the host to the device, and to lower memory resources such as L2/L1 caches. Since deep neural networks comprise compute-intensive nested loops, they often require an essential compiler optimization technique, known as loop nest optimization [23–25], to maximize data reuse in lower levels of memory hierarchies, and attain high hardware utilization. TVM also performs loop optimization, mainly to automatically search optimal schedules for partial loop unrolling, fully unrolling, loop interchange, fusion, and explore loop tiling options, *etc*.

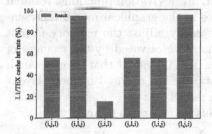 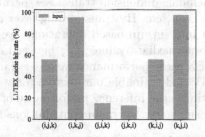

(a) Cache hit rates *vs*. output memory format permutations.

(b) Cache hit rates *vs*. input memory format permutations.

Fig. 1. L1/TEX cache hit rate performance statistics can change drastically in compiled kernels of the computation in (1) with varying input/output memory formats (b) and (a) represent separate changes we can make to the input and output formats, and each bar denotes a unique permutation. The original dimensions of input and weight tensors are $(i, j, k) = (100, 196, 512)$ and $(k, l) = (512, 784)$ respectively. The original result tensors are $(i, j, l) = (100, 196, 784)$

We find that different memory formats used by inputs and outputs of a layer can cause the cache statistics to change significantly, even for a simple batched matrix multiplication (BMM). By way of illustration, in (1), we implement a BMM operation using the Einstein summation notation.

$$\text{einsum}(\text{``ijk, kl -> ijl''}, \text{input}, \text{weight}).\tag{1}$$

Here, "ijk" and "kl" respectively denote the inputs of this operation, namely the input and weight tensors, "ijl" indicates the output shape of the evaluated result, "ijk, kl -> ijl" means that we multiply all elements along "i", "j" and "l" axes, and reduce by summation along the "k" axis, as the dimension "k" is not present in the output.

This presents us a flexible way to easily permute the input and output dimensions, and observe the impact of permutations on the performance of the resulting CUDA kernel after compilation. As shown in (1), the shapes of input and weight tensors of the BMM operation are $(100, 196, 512)$ and $(512, 784)$ respectively, and thus it computes an output of shape $(100, 196, 784)$. In memory, these values are often represented with contiguous memory arrays, and thus there are respectively 6, 2, and 6 permutations of its input, weight, and output tensor layouts. For instance, by assuming different permutations of memory formats, we find that using the original layout of the result tensor, $(i, j, l) = (100, 196, 784)$, the L1/TEX cache hit rate is surprisingly lower than assuming layouts of either (i, l, j) and (j, l, i) for the output tensor, as in Fig. 1(a). Moreover, we can see L1/TEX cache statistics also, change as we vary the input tensor formats (Fig. 1(b)).

As shown in (1), we can implement BMM with the einsum operator, this can be easily generalized to many of the layers used by transformer-based models, including dimension transposes/permutations, activation functions, residual connections, *etc.* By transforming layer nodes in the graphical model representation into einsum-based operations, we can easily adjust the memory format of all intermediate values (IV) between all nodes. Motivated by the changes of L1/TEX cache performance we observe in Fig. 1, it is evident that we can search each IV and trainable parameters (or weights) for the optimal memory layout to optimize the inference performance of the model.

In summary, our main contributions in this paper are as follows:

- We introduce a novel inter-layer compiler optimization to optimize the deep learning model. This method focuses on the tensor memory formats of trained weights and intermediate activation values in the model.
- We propose to represent the computations as einsum operations in the core modules of transformer-based models. This enables us to optimize the model by easily permuting of intermediate values. We also present a novel algorithm to explore this search space efficiently.
- We present a case study where we apply our method to MLP-Mixer, a transformer-based model. For an MLP-Mixer with 42 mixer blocks, we can achieve 23.7% inference performance enhancement when deployed in TVM on NVIDIA Tesla V100 GPU.

2   Related Works

2.1   Image Transformers

As mentioned in the previous article, most of the influential work in computer vision relies on CNNs. Nevertheless, from 2017 onwards, the researcher turned their attention to Transformers. Transformers, created by Google in 2017, initially make a significant breakthrough in the field of natural language processing [6–10].

The main structure of the transformer is the attention module, which can integrate the information of whole sentences to a specified location. The transformer model has two main contributions. One is the introduction of multi-headed attention (MHA) [26] based on the attention mechanism.

In the computer vision field, the mainstream deep vision architecture uses deep neural layers to extract features from image data, divided into information extraction for specific spatial locations and across different spatial locations [15]. Previously, this relies on CNN; the ViT [11] model first introduces the transformer structure into the CV domain, which ultimately abandoned the CNN structure in the CV domain and used the transformer structure entirely and performed well on large-scale datasets.

In addition, MLP-Mixer provides an implementation of self-attention using MLP, which surprisingly achieve good results. Figure 2 shows the structure of the MLP-Mixer. Their key contribution is the mixer modules, *i.e.* the *token-mixing* and *channel-mixing* layers. The implementations of these mixing layers are also simple and is achieved by two fully connections in the MLP module on the left side of Fig. 2. Suppose the input is X, the token-mixing MLP which acts on columns of X (performed by a transposed input $X^{\top}$). Moreover, the channel-mixing applies to each column of X.

We provide a definition for the mixer block in (2):

$$\begin{aligned}
\mathbf{U}_{*,i} &= \mathbf{X}_{*,i} + \mathbf{W}_2 \sigma \left(\mathbf{W}_1 \, \text{LayerNorm}(\mathbf{X})_{*,i} \right), \\
\mathbf{Y}_{j,*} &= \mathbf{U}_{j,*} + \mathbf{W}_4 \sigma \left(\mathbf{W}_3 \, \text{LayerNorm}(\mathbf{U})_{j,*} \right),
\end{aligned} \tag{2}$$

where i, j are in the ranges $[1, C]$ and $[1, S]$ respectively and σ represents an element-wise nonlinearity (*e.g.* GELU [27] by default). S means the number of image patches, ans C represents the hidden dimension of mixer layers. $\mathbf{W}_1$ and $\mathbf{W}_2$ represent the weight matrix in the token-mixing module. $\mathbf{W}_3$ and $\mathbf{W}_4$ represent the weight matrix in the channel-mixing module. Furthermore, in the MLP-Mixer model, D_S and D_C are defined as the number of hidden neuron numbers in the token-mixing and channel-mixing MLPs. We can get the data matrix from token-mixing module as $\mathbf{U}_{*,i}$, and then as input data flow into channel-mixing module to get $\mathbf{Y}_{j,*}$.

The input of every layer in the mixer model is the same size so that it has an optimization space in the mixer layer. In addition, mixer also use skip-connections [2] and layer normalization [28]. Moreover, mixer architecture uses a global average pooling layer and then a linear classifier at the end.

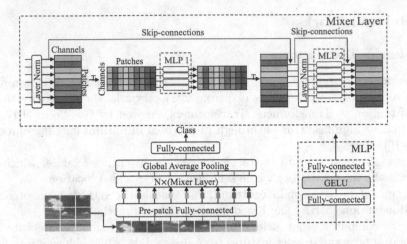

Fig. 2. MLP-Mixer architecture.

2.2   GPU Architecture

Compute Unified Device Architecture (CUDA), developed by NVIDIA, is a parallel computing platform and application programming interface for GPUs [29]. When accelerating deep learning models on sophisticated device memory hierarchy, full use of memory and computation units can achieve the best training or inference performance. As an example, the Tesla V100 GPU features the Volta GV100 GPU micro-architecture, which contains 84 parallel streaming multiprocessors (SMs). Figure 3 shows the Tesla V100 GPU architecture, which has 80 SMs that can operate in parallel. The architecture also comprises many different levels of memory hierarchy. There are four processing blocks for each SM. Every processing block possesses a 256 KB register file, and an SM (4 blocks) can configure up to 96 KB of shared memory. Threads in the same thread block will execute the same code but with different data, following the Single Instruction Multiple Thread (SIMT) mechanism in NVIDIA GPUs.

2.3   Compiler Optimizations

A compiler is a computer program that converts the code written in a specific programming language into target code, *i.e.*, machine code that can be executed directly on the target hardware platform. It provides an abstraction of program functionality, and automatic code optimizations to leverage the target hardware resources effectively. Deep learning compilers thus use a similar idea to solve the problem that different deep learning frameworks have to correspond to specific acceleration frameworks, simplifying and optimizing the porting of deep learning models to hardware platforms.

Today's DL frameworks, *e.g.* PyTorch, TensorFlow, and Caffe, performs only graph-level optimization when deploying models, and make use of existing CUDA

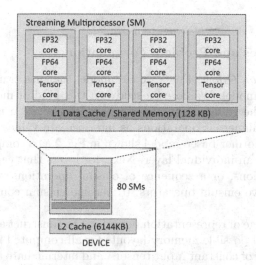

Fig. 3. Tesla V100 GPU architecture [30]

kernel libraries for computations on GPUs, and are thus often unable to perform operator-level optimizations for specific hardware backends. Therefore, in recent years, traditional compiler ideas and code generation techniques have been introduced into deep learning deployment tools to simplify the porting of deep learning models to specific hardware platforms and optimize model performance.

As computationally intensive programs are typically structured as sequences of nested loops, existing compiler optimizations focus on making nested loops run faster. Deep learning applications also follow this pattern with well-structured computations. Loop optimization techniques frequently used in parallelizing compilers today include loop interchange, loop fusion, loop distribution or loop fission and unimodular transformation, and loop tiling [31]. All of these loop optimization techniques refactor loop structures in the program and reorder instances of memory accesses and statements within the loop to improve the parallelism of program execution.

TVM is an automated, end-to-end deep learning compiler that introduces hardware-oriented low-level code-level optimization techniques on top of the many computational graph-oriented optimization techniques. Such a two-tier optimization architecture comprises graph optimization and scheduling techniques for deep learning models, such as operator fusion and access latency hiding. TVM solves the generality problem by supporting different deep learning framework front-ends and different hardware backends through an intermediate representation (IR).

3   Method

3.1   Preliminaries and Problem Formulation

Einsum Computation Graph. First, we call model that has transformer module transformer-based model. We do case study on this kind of model as shown in Fig. 2. We define the results generated by the data between multiple network layers or between numerous operations as intermediate values (IVs). Then, we represent the transformer-based model shown in Fig. 2 as a computational graph where each node is an individual layer. Next, for layers that can be represented with einsum notations, or a sequence of einsum operations, we replace them with their respective einsum operators, to become einsum computation graph, as shown in Fig. 4.

This slight change of representation permits us to construct a complete search space containing all possible memory layouts for all computed intermediate values (IV), consisting of constant input tensors, and intermediate activation results from layers used as inputs to subsequent layers. This search aims to find the optimal performance that we can possibly attain by varying the dimension orders of all IVs. As the set of all possible combinations of permutation scales exponentially with the number of IVs, and deep learning models are typically very large, an algorithm is then introduced to search more efficiently than exhaustive enumeration.

In the Einsum computation graph, we optimize all IV layouts. Formally, we define a combination

$$C = \left\{ \left(IV_1^i \right), \left(IV_2^i \right), \dots, \left(IV_k^i \right) \right\}, \tag{3}$$

where IV_i^j represents a layout permutation for the IV, and IV^i means one of all layout possibilities of the i-th Einsum/Einops layer.

Problem Formulation. Given a search space S which contains all the IVs layout possibilities from the Einsum computation graph and C represents the IV layout combination. Suppose $G_E(C)$ is the Einsum computation graph of C; our goal is to search for a C^*:

$$C^* = \arg \min_C \text{Cost}(G_E(C)), \tag{4}$$

where $\text{Cost}(G_E(C))$ evaluates the inference time of the TVM-compiled model $G_E(C)$, and C^* thus denotes the one with the minimum run time. Furthermore, we can represent C^* as:

$$C^* = \left\{ \left(IV_1^* \right), \left(IV_2^* \right), \dots, \left(IV_k^* \right) \right\}, \tag{5}$$

where IV_k^* means the layout in the i-th phase Einsum/Einops layer makes the model the best inference performance.

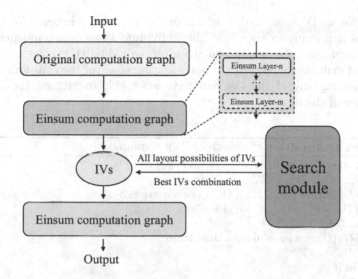

Fig. 4. Einsum computation graph.

As we use Einsum operators to implement computations in the transformer-based model, it provides us with the flexibility of changing the ordering of dimensions used by the IVs. For instance, given a fully connected layer, where the input data of the shape $(100, 196, 768)$ and the weight of $(768, 512)$, we can use (6) to calculate a result with shape $(100, 196, 512)$. If we want to permute the dimensions of the result tensor to be a $(196, 100, 512)$, we just need to change the Einsum operation from (6) to (7) for this layer:

$$\text{einsum}(\text{``ijl, lk -> ijk''}, \text{input}, \text{weight}). \tag{6}$$

$$\text{einsum}(\text{``ijl, lk -> jik''}, \text{input}, \text{weight}). \tag{7}$$

Note that subsequent layers that use the result tensor are also expected to change their input dimension orders to ensure the correctness of computation.

The search space contains all IV combinations, as expressed in (3). In all the possibilities, we need to find those combinations which makes the model inference time minimum as expressed in (4). When the overall L1/TEX cache hit rate of each computational module inside the Einsum computational graph reaches the highest, the inference speed of the model achieves the fastest speed.

3.2   Search Algorithm

We found that when we change the layout of one of the IVs in the Einsum computation graph, the hit rate of the L1/TEX cache of the GPU kernel function responsible for the IV computation changes, as we described in the previous section. When the hit rate of the L1/TEX cache is high, it makes the computation less time-consuming. Therefore, we try to use the greedy strategy to try

to search for an IV combination which makes inference performance enhancement. It is important to note that the individual IVs are not independent of
each other, changing the tensor format for an individual IV can impact the performance of multiple layers. For the optimization space of the transformer-based
model, changing any of the IVs can have a notable impact on the inference
performance of the model.

Algorithm 1. Algorithm of Searching IVs combination

1: Initialization:$C = \{(IV_1^c), (IV_2^c), \ldots, (IV_k^c)\}, c \leftarrow 0,$
2: **for** $(IV_i^c, IV_{i+1}^c, IV_{i+2}^c, IV_{i+3}^c) \in C$ **do**
3:     Fix $C - (IV_i^c, IV_{i+1}^c, IV_{i+2}^c, IV_{i+3}^c)\, randomly \in S$
4:     **for** $(IV_i^j, IV_{i+1}^k, IV_{i+2}^l, IV_{i+3}^m) \in S$ **do**
5:         run $G_E(C)$ in TVM
6:         **if** $G_E(C)$ run in minimum time **then**
7:             $IV_i^* \leftarrow IV_i^j$
8:         **end if**
9:     **end for**
10:    $C^* \leftarrow \{(IV_1^i), (IV_2^i), \ldots, (IV_k^i)\}$
11:    $i \leftarrow i + 1$
12: **end for**

Algorithm 1 shows our search strategy apart from exhaustive enumeration.
We set the policy to focus on the current Einsum/Einops layer and the impact
of the subsequent three layers on the current layer each time with the rest of
the IVs fixed to a random combination. Therefore, each time we search for the
best layout of the current IV, we change the layouts of the last three IVs at
the same time to select the layout that makes the inference performance of the
model best. For all IVs, we search with the same strategy until we get the best
combination shown in (5) which makes $G_E(C^*)$ run in the minimum time.

4   Results

4.1   Inference Performance

As a case study of the proposed optimization method, we apply it to enhance
inference performance with the transformer-based model, MLP-Mixer, jointly
with TVM's graph- and code-level optimization passes. As a transformer-based
model, MLP-Mixer uses mixing layers to implement a structure similar to the
self-attention mechanism. We can abstract the MLP-Mixer into multiple connected Einsum layers as shown in Fig. 4. For MLP-Mixer, as a multi-layer structure, it contains at least a large number of IVs. It thus forms a vast search space
of IVs, with at least $3!^3 \times 2!^5 = 6912$ options for each residual block, and for an
MLP-Mixer with d residual blocks, the search space can be as large as 6912^d.
We note that all residual blocks contain identical computation patterns, and
it is reasonable to speculate that an optimal option for one residual block can
translate well to the entire network. As it is infeasible to search the full space

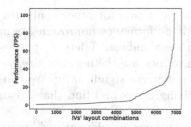

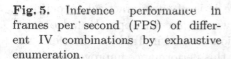

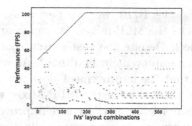

Fig. 5. Inference performance in frames per second (FPS) of different IV combinations by exhaustive enumeration.

Fig. 6. Inference performance via different IVs' layout combinations searched by Algorithm 1.

exhaustively, we instead search within the space of one residual block, with 6912 unique options.

We deploy the MLP-Mixer model on the deep learning compiler framework TVM on Tesla V100 GPU and apply our proposed optimization approach to test the model inference performance while using TVM's optimization techniques (*e.g.*, operator fusion). We summarize the specification of the MLP-Mixer shown in Table 2. For the B/16 configuration of the MLP-Mixer, suppose our input data is four-dimensional image data $(100, 3, 224, 224)$, where the first dimension represents the batch size of image data. First, we traverse the entire optimization space, showing in Fig. 5. The best performance of the B/16 MLP-mixer can be seen in Fig. 5. In Fig. 5 we arrange all layout combinations of all IVs in an increasing order of performance We implement the original MLP-mixer as a baseline model using the Einsum operator. For the B/16 MLP-Mixer, we obtain an 18% improvement in model inference speed after optimizing according to our proposed optimization approach as shown in Table 2. This validates the feasibility of our optimization approach.

Table 2. Specifications of the MLP-Mixer architectures, and speed-up after optimization.

Specification	S/16	B/16	L/16	H/16
Number of residual blocks	8	16	32	42
Hidden size C	512	768	1,024	1,280
Sequence length S	196	196	196	196
MLP dimension D_C	2,048	3,072	4,096	5,120
MLP dimension D_S	256	384	512	640
Run time before optimization (ms)	558	1,109	2,211	2,900
Run time after optimization (ms)	506	938	1,808	2,344
Speed-up	10.2%	18.2%	22.2%	23.7%

Besides B/16, we also performed an exhaustive search for other configurations of the MLP-mixer. We summarize all their performance improvements in Table 2. Despite the vast search space, we can see significant inference performance improvement in Table 2. As we continue to increase the network size, we find that the improvement does not continue to increase significantly. We continue the test with the MLP-Mixer with 42 mixing layers and find that it can achieve a 1.23× performance improvement.

However, we must recompile the model every time we deploy a different IV combination option in TVM. Therefore it is often impractical to perform an exhaustive search. At the same time, we can see an upper bound on the performance improvement of our optimization method in Table 2. Therefore, we propose an alternative search strategy with this performance improvement limit as a premise. We search this optimization space according to Algorithm 1. We can see from Fig. 6 that we reduce the number of searches significantly and also reach an upper limit of performance similar to that of the exhaustive search strategy.

This optimization algorithm also benefits from our verified upper limit of performance improvement. Although we show an overview of over 500 search times in Fig. 6, the more searches we have, the closer we get to the upper limit of performance improvement according to Algorithm 1. Therefore, when using our proposed search method, the number of searches can be chosen according to the actual situation.

4.2 Analyses

As mentioned earlier, our optimization approach is specific to the tensor memory format. When performing matrix operations, access to the data does not mean that access to the original data format is the best. Every matrix operation has a data format suitable for the current operation, which is the foundation for optimizing the transformer model in this article. The proper data format enables the model to run on the GPU with a high hit rate of the GPU's L1/TEX cache, which speeds up the inference performance of the deep learning model.

The architecture of the Tesla V100 GPU is a multi-tier memory architecture frame. The L1/TEX cache is the closest storage structure to the computation unit, and the higher its hit rate, with less time spent on data transfer during the computation. We tested the hit rate of the L1/TEX cache before and after optimization for MLP-Mixer with B/16 specification.

As shown in Fig. 7, We can see that the hit rate of the L1/TEX cache significantly improves after optimization, which is the key to inference performance improvement. In the mixing layer, we consider the effect of an IV change on both the output of the current Einsum layer and the input of the next Einsum layer. We can see from Fig. 7 that for the token-mixing module and channel-mixing module, the L1/TEX cache performance of their main computation kernel improves significantly after the optimization compared to before.

The present optimization selects a data format suitable for matrix operations without more CUDA programming. As a result, the access to the data in TVM

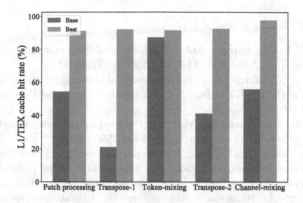

Fig. 7. L1/TEX cache performance in different modules in MLP-Mixer with B/16 specification.

is more appropriate to the needs of the computation, which in turn speeds up the inference process of the model.

5   Conclusion

In this paper, we find that for matrix operations on the GPU, changing the memory layout of the input and output tensors of the operation results in an increase in the hit rates of the L1/TEX cache of the kernel responsible for the calculation. This observation allows us to speed up inference in existing deep learning models. We thus present a new compiler optimization pass, which first abstracts the transformer-based model into a computational graph and replaces feasible layers with Einsum-based variants. This enables us to permute the dimension order of intermediate values in the graph, in order to optimize the performance of kernels compiled from the changed Einsum operations. Based on a case study of exhaustive enumeration on a residual block in MLP-Mixer, we discover the best combination of IV memory layouts after the search that can improve the inference speed by up to 23.7% for an MLP-Mixer model with 42 mixing residual blocks. As exhaustive search is often impractical, we propose a new algorithm for the search space of IVs, which can reduce the number of searched options significantly and make similar improvements to exhaustive enumeration. Finally, we present and analyze a comparison of the cache hit rate statistics before and after optimization.

Acknowledgment. This work is supported in part by National Key R&D Program of China (No. 2019YFB2102100), Key-Area Research and Development Program of Guangdong Province (No. 2020B010164003), and Shenzhen Science and Technology Innovation Commission (No. JCYJ20190812160003719 and JCYJ20220531100804-009).

References

1. Sejnowski, T.J.: The unreasonable effectiveness of deep learning in artificial intelligence. Proc. Natl. Acad. Sci. **117**(48), 30033–30038 (2020)
2. He, K., Zhang, X., Ren, S., Sun, J.: Deep residual learning for image recognition. In: Proceedings of the IEEE Conference on Computer Vision and Pattern Recognition, pp. 770–778 (2016)
3. Simonyan, K., Zisserman, A.: Very deep convolutional networks for large-scale image recognition. arXiv preprint arXiv:1409.1556 (2014)
4. Szegedy, C., Vanhoucke, V., Ioffe, S., Shlens, J., Wojna, Z.: Rethinking the inception architecture for computer vision. In: Proceedings of the IEEE Conference on Computer Vision and Pattern Recognition, pp. 2818–2826 (2016)
5. Vaswani, A., et al.: Attention is all you need. In: Advances in Neural Information Processing Systems, vol. 30 (2017)
6. Lee, J.D.M.C.K., Toutanova, K.: Pre-training of deep bidirectional transformers for language understanding. arXiv preprint arXiv:1810.04805 (2018)
7. Yang, Z., Dai, Z., Yang, Y., Carbonell, J., Salakhutdinov, R.R., Le, Q.V.: XLNet: generalized autoregressive pretraining for language understanding. In: Advances in Neural Information Processing Systems, vol. 32 (2019)
8. Liu, Y., et al.: RoBERTa: a robustly optimized BERT pretraining approach. arXiv preprint arXiv:1907.11692 (2019)
9. Raffel, C., et al.: Exploring the limits of transfer learning with a unified text-to-text transformer. J. Mach. Learn. Res. **21**(140), 1–67 (2020)
10. Brown, T., et al.: Language models are few-shot learners. In: Advances in Neural Information Processing Systems, vol. 33, pp. 1877–1901 (2020)
11. Dosovitskiy, A., et al.: An image is worth 16×16 words: transformers for image recognition at scale. arXiv preprint arXiv:2010.11929 (2020)
12. Touvron, H., Cord, M., Douze, M., Massa, F., Sablayrolles, A., Jégou, H.: Training data-efficient image transformers & distillation through attention. In: International Conference on Machine Learning, pp. 10347–10357. PMLR (2021)
13. Carion, N., Massa, F., Synnaeve, G., Usunier, N., Kirillov, A., Zagoruyko, S.: End-to-end object detection with transformers. In: Vedaldi, A., Bischof, H., Brox, T., Frahm, J.-M. (eds.) ECCV 2020. LNCS, vol. 12346, pp. 213–229. Springer, Cham (2020). https://doi.org/10.1007/978-3-030-58452-8_13
14. Liu, Z., et al.: Swin transformer: hierarchical vision transformer using shifted windows. In: Proceedings of the IEEE/CVF International Conference on Computer Vision, pp. 10012–10022 (2021)
15. Tolstikhin, I.O., et al.: MLP-mixer: an all-MLP architecture for vision. In: Advances in Neural Information Processing Systems, vol. 34, pp. 24261–24272 (2021)
16. Paszke, A., et al.: Automatic differentiation in PyTorch (2017)
17. Abadi, M., et al.: TensorFlow: a system for large-scale machine learning. In: 12th USENIX Symposium on Operating Systems Design and Implementation (OSDI 2016), pp. 265–283 (2016)
18. Jia, Y., et al.: Caffe: convolutional architecture for fast feature embedding. In: Proceedings of the 22nd ACM International Conference on Multimedia, pp. 675–678 (2014)
19. Chen, T., et al.: TVM: an automated end-to-end optimizing compiler for deep learning. In: 13th USENIX Symposium on Operating Systems Design and Implementation (OSDI 2018), pp. 578–594 (2018)

20. Cyphers, S., et al.: Intel nGraph: an intermediate representation, compiler, and executor for deep learning. arXiv preprint arXiv:1801.08058 (2018)
21. Vasilache, N., et al.: Tensor comprehensions: framework-agnostic high-performance machine learning abstractions. arXiv preprint arXiv:1802.04730 (2018)
22. Mudigere, D.: Data access optimized applications on the GPU using NVIDIA CUDA. Master's thesis, Technische Universität München (2009)
23. Bondhugula, U., Hartono, A., Ramanujam, J., Sadayappan, P.: A practical automatic polyhedral parallelizer and locality optimizer. In: Proceedings of the 29th ACM SIGPLAN Conference on Programming Language Design and Implementation, pp. 101–113 (2008)
24. Kudlur, M., Mahlke, S.: Orchestrating the execution of stream programs on multicore platforms. ACM SIGPLAN Not. **43**(6), 114–124 (2008)
25. Pouchet, L.N., et al.: Loop transformations: convexity, pruning and optimization. ACM SIGPLAN Not. **46**(1), 549–562 (2011)
26. Zheng, S., et al.: Rethinking semantic segmentation from a sequence-to-sequence perspective with transformers. In: Proceedings of the IEEE/CVF Conference on Computer Vision and Pattern Recognition, pp. 6881–6890 (2021)
27. Hendrycks, D., Gimpel, K.: Gaussian error linear units (GELUs). arXiv preprint arXiv:1606.08415 (2016)
28. Ba, J.L., Kiros, J.R., Hinton, G.E.: Layer normalization arXiv preprint arXiv:1607.06450 (2016)
29. NVIDIA, Vingelmann, P., Fitzek, F.H.: CUDA, release: 10.2.89 (2020)
30. Lindholm, E., Nickolls, J., Oberman, S., Montrym, J.: NVIDIA Tesla: a unified graphics and computing architecture. IEEE Micro **28**(2), 39–55 (2008)
31. Srikant, Y., Shankar, P.: The Compiler Design Handbook: Optimizations and Machine Code Generation. CRC Press, Boca Raton (2018)

Improving Few-Shot Image Classification with Self-supervised Learning

Shisheng Deng[1,2], Dongping Liao[3], Xitong Gao[1(✉)], Juanjuan Zhao[1], and Kejiang Ye[1]

[1] Shenzhen Institute of Advanced Technology, Chinese Academy of Sciences, Shenzhen 518000, China
{ss.deng,xt.gao,jj.zhao,kj.ye}@siat.ac.cn
[2] University of Chinese Academy of Sciences, Beijing 100049, China
[3] University of Macau, Macau SAR 999078, China
yb97428@umac.mo

Abstract. Few-Shot Image Classification (FSIC) aims to learn an image classifier with only a few training samples. The key challenge of few-shot image classification is to learn this classifier with scarce labeled data. To tackle the issue, we leverage the self-supervised learning (SSL) paradigm to exploit unsupervised information. This work builds upon two-stage training paradigm, to push the current state-of-the-art (SOTA) in solving FSIC problem further. Specifically, we incorporate the traditional self-supervised learning method (TSSL) into the pre-training stage and propose an episodic contrastive loss (CL) as an auxiliary supervision for the meta-training stage. The proposed bipartite method, called FSIC-SSL, can SOTA task accuracies on two mainstream FSIC benchmark datasets. Our code will be available at https://github.com/SethDeng/FSIC_SSL.

Keywords: Few-shot image classification · Self-supervised learning · Contrastive learning

1 Introduction

Over the last decade, Deep Neural Networks (DNN) [29,67,68] have achieved great or even better performance than human on a variety of vision tasks. However, due to its data-driven nature, DNNs are less likely to excel in scenarios with sparse labeled data. Yet in practice, owing to privacy, security ethics and cost issues, it is difficult to collect and label large and comprehensive datasets which are exclusive to certain domains (*i.e.* healthcare and public safety). The human's capability to learn novel concepts from a few samples motivates the advancement of a new machine learning paradigm [19,20], namely few-shot learning (FSL), which aims to train DNNs with a limited number of samples per task when given a dataset of such tasks.

S. Deng and D. Liao—Equal contribution.

K. Ye and L.-J. Zhang (Eds.): CLOUD 2022, LNCS 13731, pp. 54–68, 2022.
https://doi.org/10.1007/978-3-031-23498-9_5

Bridging the gap between data-driven machine learning and data-scarce scenarios is a fruitful research direction. FSL enables a broad range of scenarios for real-world applications [58] (*i.e.*, image classification [57], identify new drugs [2], character generation [35], advanced robotics [15], language modeling [14], video event detection [61], *etc.*).

Among these applications, few-shot image classification (FSIC) is a sub-field of few-shot learning and a scenario most commonly used to benchmark the performance of few-shot learning algorithms.

According to previous studies, we can broadly consider few-shot image classification scenario from the data-augment [31] and knowledge-transfer [65] perspectives, each with its respective approaches.

In this paper, we focus on the methods in which data augmentation can be made more effective. Many prior works use self-supervised learning (SSL) [8, 24,66], and contrastive learning (CL) [10,28], as effective data-augmentation strategies. However, the potential of SSL and CL in FSIC remains relatively unexplored. Among the existing researches, some use traditional SSL [51,52], while others employ CL [13,39,63]. To fully utilize traditional SSL and CL in FSIC, we propose a new data-augment method, called **FSIC-SSL**, to leverage the merits from both worlds.

Recently, numerous studies [11,17,44,55] show that the two-stage training paradigm, consisting of a pre-training stage and a meta-training stage, is effective in attaining SOTA performance In FSIC. However, in this regular two-stage training paradigm, it only minimizes the standard cross-entropy loss (CE) with labels from train-set, either in pre-training or meta-training stage.

Our proposed method, FSIC-SSL, applies traditional self-supervised learning and contrastive learning to the pre-training and meta-training stage, respectively. First, in the pre-training stage, we take the SSL objective (*i.e.*, predicting rotations in augmented images) as an auxiliary loss to train the feature extractor. With the benefits of SSL, our feature extractor is able to learn more domain knowledge from limited number of samples. Second, in the meta-training stage, we introduce a contrastive loss as pretext task supervision to extract generalizable representation. Specifically, we obtain the positive and negative samples in contrastive learning by performing 2D cropping, gray-scale transformation and contrast manipulations of the original image.

FSIC-SSL combines the advantages of self-supervised learning and contrastive learning effectively in the two stages training framework of FSL, allowing the model to learn meta-knowledge, which plays a crucial role in identifying novel classes. In this paper, we show that FSIC-SSL can help the current SOTA method, DeepEMD, to achieve new SOTAs on popular FSIC benchmark datasets.

The key contributions of this paper can be summarized as follows:

- To the best of our knowledge, we propose the first FSIC method that can take advantage of both self-supervised learning and contrastive learning.
- Experiment results show that our method, FSIC-SSL, pushes the current SOTA on mainstream FSIC benchmark datasets (*i.e. mini*-ImageNet, *tiered*-ImageNet).

2   Background and Related Work

2.1   Few-Shot Image Classification (FSIC)

Few-shot learning (FSL) aims to learn a model with strong generalization ability from a limited number of samples. Few-shot image classification (FSIC) has numerous application scenarios, among which, FSIC is the most popular scenario for evaluating FSL algorithms.

Few-Shot Image Classification (FSIC). A FSIC task can be defined as $\mathcal{D}_{\text{FSIC}} = \{\mathcal{D}_{\text{train}}, \mathcal{D}_{\text{test}}\}$, where$\{y \mid (x, y) \in \mathcal{D}_{\text{train}}\} \cap \{y \mid (x, y) \in \mathcal{D}_{\text{test}}\} = \emptyset$, *i.e.*, the test and train datasets do not contain common labels. Following [35], most of the recent works on FSIC employ the standard *N-way K-shot (M-query)* episodic task learning.

Specifically, for each FSIC task, we sample n episodic tasks $\{T_1, \ldots, T_n\}$ from $\mathcal{D}_{\text{train}}$ as training episodes, and m episodic tasks $\{T_1, \ldots, T_m\}$ from $\mathcal{D}_{\text{test}}$ as testing episodes. Each episodic task T_i consists of a support set T_i^S and a query set T_i^Q. From a dataset, each episodic tasks randomly samples N categories respectively, with each category sampling K image-label pairs (x, y), $T_i^S = \{(x_k, y_k)_{k=1}^{N \times K}\}$ for support set, and each category sampling M image-label pairs (x, y), $T_i^Q = \{(x_k, y_k)_{k=1}^{N \times M}\}$ for query set. Both $\mathcal{D}_{\text{train}}$ and $\mathcal{D}_{\text{test}}$ samples the support and query sets following the above configuration, except the $\mathcal{D}_{\text{test}}$ provides no labels for the query set, namely, $T_i^Q = \{(x_k)_{k=1}^{N \times M}\}$.

As Table 1 shows, current FSIC approaches could be broadly divided into two categories: *data-augment based*, and *knowledge-transfer based*.

Table 1. An overview of few-shot image classification methods

Perspective		
Data-augment	Auxiliary-data	PMF [31], CNAPS+FETI [5], EP [49], *etc.*
	Unlabeled-data	SITD [13], FSL-SSL [51], PN+CL [39], *etc.*
	Generated-data	MatchGan [30], FSGAN [1], CGAN [47],etc.
Knowledge-transfer	Metric	DeepEMD [65], FEAT [64], TADAM [44], *etc.*
	Meta-learning	MAML [21], MAML++ [3], Reptile [42], *etc.*
	Graph	FSL-GNN [22], DPGN [62], EGNN [34], *etc.*

Data-Augment-Based FSIC Method. The inherent challenge of FSIC is that only few samples are available in each task, resulting in low sample diversity. Data augmentation [50] is the process of performing random but realistic image transformations to improve sample diversity when data quantities are limited. It is often used to prevent model overfitting and helps DNNs generalize better. Data-augment based FSIC method could be further divided into three types: *auxiliary-data based*, *unlabeled-data based* and *generated-data based*.

Auxiliary-data based methods utilize publicly available labeled datasets(*i.e.* ImageNet [16]) in the model-training phase. Unlabeled-data based methods extend original datasets with unlabeled data. (*i.e.*, with additional training objective such as rotation prediction [24], relative patch location [43,59], image clustering [8,9] or contrastive information [4,10,27,28,60]). Generated-data based methods refer to using the generative model (*i.e.* GAN [25]) to synthesize new labeled data to augment the training data.

Knowledge-Transfer Based FSIC Method. It is widely acknowledged that knowledge transfer [26] is a major mechanism which allows humans to learn novel and complex concepts rapidly when given only few training samples. Following the various means of knowledge transfer, we roughly subdivide knowledge-transfer based FSIC methods into three categories: *metric based, meta-learning based* and *graph based*. Metric based method typically consists of two modules: an embedding module and a measurement module, where a pair of samples is first embedded into vector space by the embedding module, and then the similarity of the pair is calculated by the measurement module. Meta-learning is known as learning to learn [53]. Meta-learning enables models to obtain a learning capability that allows them to automatically learn meta-knowledge [56] (*i.e.*, the model's hyperparameters, the initialization of the DNN). Specifically, meta-learning based methods optimizes a bi-level objective to find optimal initial parameters for FSIC episodic tasks. Graph based method constructs a graph of all the samples in an episodic task to learn to classify, where the nodes in the graph are the samples while the edges of the graph are the similarities of two inter-connected samples.

In fact, the above methods are not mutually exclusive, and methods may be used simultaneously to improve performance.

2.2 Self-Supervised Learning (SSL)

Labeling data is costly and difficult to scale up. For this reason, there is a growing interest in learning representations from unlabeled data. In contrast to supervised learning approaches which requires manually-labeled data, self-supervised learning is trained with unlabeled data and automatically generates pseudo-labels based on a predefined pretext task, without any manual annotation.

Traditional Self-Supervised Learning (TSSL). In the context of image classification tasks, Jing et al. [33] summarize the self-supervised pretext tasks into two categories: *generation-based* [25,66] and *context-based* [24,43] methods.

Generation-based methods learn features by tackling pretextual tasks concerning with image generation, such as image colorization [66], image super resolution [36], image inpainting [46] and image generation with GAN [25].

Context-based methods extract features through contextual information of images, such as context similarity (*e.g.*, image clustering [8,9]), spatial structure (*e.g.*, image jigsaw puzzle [43,59], image rotation prediction [24]).

We describe these self-supervised methods, which exploit the original characteristics of each image, as traditional self-supervised method.

Contrastive Learning (CL). The concept of contrastive learning is developed based on the the idea that humans not only learn from positive signals, but can also benefit from correcting undesirable patterns of behavior.

Recently, contrastive learning has become one of the most popular paradigms for self-supervised visual representation learning.

CL methods commonly construct contrastive pairs of instances with various data augmentations and optimize the contrastive loss aiming to keep the instances close for the positive pairs (the original image and the images obtained from the original image through data augmentations), whereas steering away from the negative pairs (*i.e.*, other images) in the embedding space.

Hadsell et al. [27] proposed contrastive learning for the first time. More recently, Wu et al. [60] took instance discrimination into consideration and used noisy contrastive loss to learn representations. Tian et al. [54] considered that different views of an image (*i.e.* grayscale map, semantic segmentation map) representing the same image should be positive pairs of each other, other images not matching on the view should be treated as negative pairs. SimCLR [10] summarized the standard framework for contrast learning and shows the effect of different combinations of two random view transformations. However, there is a drawback that its performance is dependent on large batches. MoCo [28] constructed a dynamic dictionary with a queue and a moving-averaged encoder. This allows building a large and consistent dictionary dynamically, thus addressing the over-consumption of resources in CL models.

Since the batch size of episodic task is relatively small, we employ MoCo's framework into our model.

2.3 Few-Shot Image Classification with Self-Supervised Learning

SSL enables a model to learn unsupervised information from labeled data. Meanwhile, FSIC tasks have only a few labeled training examples. The combination of FSIC and SSL has thus gained notable traction in recent years.

Compared to the works [12,23,51,52] that bring traditional self-supervised methods (*i.e.* rotation prediction, relative patch location) to FSL as auxiliary losses, the current approaches is focused on exploring the applicability of contrastive loss in FSIC.

Doersch et al. [18] first introduced SimCLR, while Chen et al. [13] utilized MoCo contrastive learning method to FSIC task for a more general feature representation. Luo et al. [39] trained a network to crop the optimal sample pairs, Ma et al. [40] employed supervised contrastive loss to train the feature extractor. Ouali et al. [45] brought in spatial contrast loss (*i.e.*, the loss is calculated separately on different channels of the image and then summarized). Liu et al. [37] masked an image randomly before generating positive and negative sample pairs from the masked image. Yang et al. [63] used contrastive loss in the two stages of training, separately.

Different from the previous work, our proposed approach, FSIC-SSL, integrates traditional self-supervised learning and contrastive learning in FSIC. In the pre-training stage, we take traditional SSL (rotation prediction) as an auxiliary loss to train the feature extractor. With the help of traditional SSL, our feature extractor is able to learn more domain knowledge from the same-number of samples. In the meta-training stage, we introduce contrastive loss as pretext task to extract generalizable representations.

3 Methodology

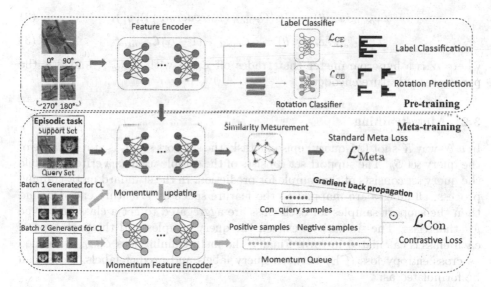

Fig. 1. Structure of our proposed FSIC-SSL for two-stage training method. In the pre-training stage, we learn a feature encoder with original image and four-angle rotated images on the training set. In meta-training stages, to facilitate the standard meta-training process, we employ the feature extractor trained in pre-training stage for standard meta-training, while using two batches of images that are generated from the images of episodic task for contrastive learning. Here we take *2-way 1-shot (2-query)* classification task as an example for illustration, and ⊙ means dot product.

As Fig. 1 shows, our FSIC-SSL employs traditional self-supervised learning method (rotation prediction) and contrastive learning method (MoCo) on two training phases separately, to enhance the performance of the model. Note that we take DeepEMD [65], the current SOTA FSIC method, as our baseline. In the following subsections, we will introduce our framework in detail.

3.1 Pre-training

To mitigate the training overfitting problem of feature encoder, caused by the standard label classification alone, we introduce rotation prediction as a pretext task in the pre-training phase.

We follow the setting of [52], where the input image is rotated by the four angle ($0°$, $90°$, $180°$, $270°$). We denote the original image as x_i, the image lable as y_i, the oriented image as x_i^r, and the oriented target as y_i^r. Both label calssifier C_{lable} and rotation classifier C_{rotate} are fully connected neural networks. Notably, we use cross entropy loss (CE) as the loss function in both lable classification and rotation prediction.

Consequently, the loss function for pre-training stage can be expressed as:

$$\mathcal{L}_{label}(x_i, \theta) = CE(C_{label}(Encoder_\theta(x_i)), y_i), \tag{1}$$

$$\mathcal{L}_{rotate}(x_i^r, \theta) = CE(C_{rotate}(Encoder_\theta(x_i^r)), y_i^r), \tag{2}$$

$$\mathcal{L}_{pretrain}(x_i, x_i^r, \theta) = \alpha\mathcal{L}_{label} + (1 - \alpha)\mathcal{L}_{rotate}, \tag{3}$$

where α is a hyperparameter that trades off $\mathcal{L}_{label}$ with $\mathcal{L}_{rotate}$, and θ is the parameter of feature encoder.

3.2 Meta-training

In a N-way K-shot (M-query) episodic task, the support set $\mathcal{S}_s$ is at a distance of the query set $\mathcal{S}_q$. The support set consists of the sample used as a criterion while the query set consists of the sample for prediction. In the standard meta-training process, all images are mapped to the feature space by a feature encoder, and then the support samples for each class are aggregated to get a class prototype for that class. The similarity between the query samples and the prototype of each class is calculated in turn. Finally, the meta-training loss $\mathcal{L}_{meta}$ is defined as cross entropy loss (CE) between query labels and predict labels. These can be formulated as:

$$P_i = Aggregate_{y=i}(Encoder_\theta(x)), (x, y) \in \mathcal{S}_s, \tag{4}$$

$$\hat{y} = \underset{argmin}{Sim}(Encoder_\theta(x), P_i), (x, y) \in \mathcal{S}_q, \tag{5}$$

$$\mathcal{L}_{meta}(\mathcal{S}_s, \mathcal{S}_q, \theta) = \frac{1}{NM} \sum_{(x,y)\in\mathcal{S}_q} CE(\hat{y}, y), \tag{6}$$

where P_i is the prototype of each class, Sim is the similarity metric, $\hat{y}$ is the predict lable, and θ is the parameter of feature encoder.

In contrast to the standard meta-training process, we employ improved MoCo, a contrastive learning method, as an auxiliary task to enhance the performance of the model in meta-training stages.

There are several key steps involved in this auxiliary task:

- We obtain two batches of images that are generated from the images of episodic task by 2D cropping, rotation, horizontal flip, grayscale transformation and contrast control of the original image, *etc.*
- We use the feature encoder to map one of the batches to the feature space as con_query features (to distinguish it from the query features in standard meta-learning process). We simultaneously leverage momentum feature encoder to map another batch to the feature space as positive features, while those that are not generated via images in this episodic task are negative samples. The parameters of momentum feature encoder evolve dynamically with feature encoder. Formally,

$$\omega \leftarrow m\omega + (1 - m)\theta, \tag{7}$$

here $m \in [0, 1)$ is a momentum coefficient, ω is the parameters of the momentum feature encoder, and θ is the parameters of the feature encoder.
- We create an in-and-out queue to store positive and negative features. We obtain the contrastive loss by the dot-products of con_query feature with positive feature and negative feature respectively, the contrastive loss can be formulated as:

$$\mathcal{L}_{con} = -\log \frac{\exp(con\_query \cdot positive/\tau)}{\sum_{i=0}^{Q-1} \exp(con\_query \cdot queue_i/\tau)}, \tag{8}$$

where τ is a temperature hyperparameter, and Q denotes the length of queue.
- The total loss of our proposed method can be denoted as:

$$\mathcal{L}_{meta-con} = \beta\mathcal{L}_{meta} + (1 - \beta)\mathcal{L}_{con}. \tag{9}$$

where β denotes the regularization hyperparameter for balancing two losses.

4   Experimental Results

In this section, our proposed method, FSIC-SSL, is evaluated on two FSIC benchmark datasets, *mini*-ImageNet [57] and *tiered*-ImageNet [48]. To further demonstrate the efficiency of our approach, we conducted extensive experiments using the current SOTA, DeepEMD, as our baseline.

4.1   Datasets and Baseline

***mini*-ImageNet.** One of the most popular benchmark dataset in FSIC. It is first introduced in [57], as a subset of ImageNet [16]. It contains 100 classes, with 600 color images in each class.

***tiered*-ImageNet.** Another subset of ImageNet. It contains 608 classes from 34 super-classes (779,165 images in total), with train, val and test splits, respectively containing 20, 6 and 8 super-classes [48]. In addition, since train-set and test-set belong to different super-class, the domain differences are notably larger than *mini*-ImageNet.

DeepEMD. Given a pair of images, DeepEMD, a typical metric-based method, first samples image patches from original image. Then it computes the cost matrix and the optimal matching flows, using the earth mover's distance (EMD) between pairs of features extracted from image patches. Finally, based on the optimal matching flows and cost matrix, the distance between two images could be computed exactly. In addition, in N-way K-shot (M-query) setting, when $K > 1$, DeepEMD employs a learnable embedding for each class, namely structured fully connected layer (SFC), and uses SGD to learn the parameters in the SFC, which represents the prototype of the class. The current SOTA on FSIC is a DeepEMD model that samples 25 patches uniformly from each image, and uses cosine similarity as the transportation cost between features.

4.2   Implementation Details

The pipeline of our algorithm is illustrated in Fig. 1. Following [41], we use ResNet-12 as the backbone network for the competing methods. In addition, we conduct experiments in both 5-way 1-shot and 5-way 5-shot cases on the two FSIC benchmark datasets. Additionally, in N-way K-shot (M-query) setting, a number of previous works have set the query number as 15. We analyze the query number to quantify its effect on computation overhead and accuracy. For inductive FSIC Method [32,65], 1-query is equivalent to 15-query, as query sample is independent on each other. For transductive FSIC methods [6,7,38], the query samples are dependent on each other. It is typically observed that the larger the query number, the better the classification performance. Since our method is an inductive FSIC method, we constrain the number of queries to 1 in our experiments. Our code is implemented in PyTorch, and all experiments are performed on an NVIDIA V100 GPU.

4.3   Results

Table 2 shows the comparison of performance of previous works and our proposed method on *mini*-ImageNet and *tiered*-ImageNetand we can conclude that our method outperforms previous works by a clear margin on two datasets. Remarkably, we conducted ablation experiments on the two modules of FSIC-SSL, finding that the improvements to baselines are significant for Rot or CL alone, and the combination of both may improve further.

4.4   Analysis

In the analysis section, we set the number of patches of the baseline to 9, to balance the efficiency and performance of the experiment. Note that all of the ablation experiments are conducted on *mini*-ImageNet.

Varying α in the Pre-training Stage. We first explore the hyperparameter α of the pre-training phase, α is a hyperparameter that trades off $\mathcal{L}_{label}$ with $\mathcal{L}_{rotate}$. Figure 2 shows that the classification accuracy peaks at $\alpha = 0.9$, and the blue line in Fig. 2 denote the baseline without rotation classification.

Table 2. Comparison results on *mini*-ImageNet and *tiered*-ImageNet. Results with †
are reproduced with the official implementation. All the results are with 95% confidence
interval.

Model	*mini*-ImageNet		*tiered*-ImageNet	
	1-shot	5-shot	1-shot	5-shot
TADAM [44]	58.5 ± 0.3	76.7 ± 0.3	–	–
RFS [55]	62.02 ± 0.63	79.64 ± 0.44	69.74 ± 0.72	84.41 ± 0.55
FEAT [64]	66.78 ± 0.20	82.05 ± 0.14	70.80 ± 0.23	84.79 ± 0.16
InfoPatch [37]	67.67 ± 0.45	82.44 ± 0.31	71.51 ± 0.52	85.44 ± 0.35
DeepEMD [65]	68.77 ± 0.55 †	84.13 ± 0.45 †	73.60 ± 0.54 †	86.92 ± 0.44 †
Ours (DeepEMD+Rot)	68.97 ± 0.53	83.93 ± 0.46	73.62 ± 0.53	86.93 ± 0.44
Ours (DeepEMD+CL)	69.06 ± 0.53	**84.37 ± 0.42**	**73.65 ± 0.54**	87.01 ± 0.44
Ours (DeepEMD+Rot+CL)	**69.14 ± 0.54**	84.26 ± 0.45	73.61 ± 0.54	**87.04 ± 0.43**

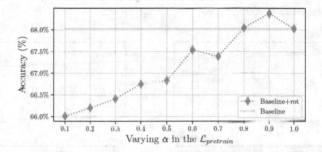

Fig. 2. Sensitivity analysis of the hyperparameter α in the pre-training stage. (Color
figure online)

Varying β in the Meta-training Stage. Similar to α, the hyperparameter β is
the regularization term weighing the standard meta-learning loss and contrastive
loss. By observing Fig. 3, we can find that when $\beta \in [0.5, 1]$, baseline with CL
is better than baseline in all cases. In contrast, Fig. 2 shows that baseline with
rotation perform better than baseline only if $\alpha = 0.8$ or 0.9. Therefore, we can
conclude that the benefit from CL to the performance improvement of the model
is better than the rotation pretext.

Changing the Length of Queue in the Meta-training Stage. Following [28], we first let the momentum coefficient $m = 0.999$, and then fix both
$\alpha = 0.9$ and $\beta = 0.7$, to explore the performance of model with various lengths
of queues. As Fig. 4a shows, surprisingly, longer queues do not always correspond to better results, as the optimal performance of model peak at the length
of queue equals 65500.

Adjusting the Momentum Coefficient m in the Meta-training Stage.
Finally, we tweak the momentum coefficient m, a hyperparameter that determines the update rate of momentum feature encoder, results are shown in Fig. 4b.

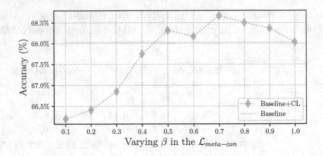

Fig. 3. Sensitivity of the hyperparameter β in meta-training stage.

As expected, the results are consistent with [28], as model reports the best performance when $m = 0.999$.

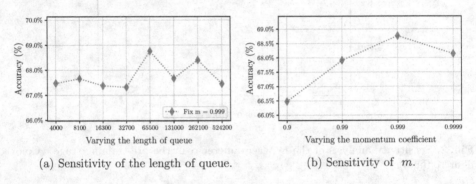

(a) Sensitivity of the length of queue.   (b) Sensitivity of m.

Fig. 4. Ablation results on (a) the length of queue and (b) the momentum coefficient m in the meta-training stage.

5   Conclusion and Future Work

In this paper, we propose a data-augment method for FSIC task. The resulting approach, FSIC-SSL, helps the current SOTA, DeepEMD, achieve new SOTA results on two mainstream benchmark datasets, *i.e.*, *mini*-ImageNet and *tiered*-ImageNet. In contrast to the previous data-augment based method, FSIC-SSL combines the benefits of self-supervised learning and contrastive learning for the first time. However, one limitation is that the computational overhead for contrastive learning is huge. Finally, we believe that this work can be further improved, especially on reducing the computational effort in learning unsupervised information.

Acknowledgment. This work is supported in part by National Key R&D Program of China (No. 2019YFB2102100), Key-Area Research and Development Program of Guangdong Province (No. 2020B010164003), and Shenzhen Science and Technology Innovation Commission (No. JCYJ20190812160003719).

References

1. Ali-Gombe, A., Elyan, E., Savoye, Y., Jayne, C.: Few-shot classifier GAN. In: 2018 International Joint Conference on Neural Networks (IJCNN), pp. 1–8. IEEE (2018)
2. Altae-Tran, H., Ramsundar, B., Pappu, A.S., Pande, V.: Low data drug discovery with one-shot learning. ACS Cent. Sci. **3**(4), 283–293 (2017)
3. Antoniou, A., Edwards, H., Storkey, A.: How to train your MAML. In: International Conference on Learning Representations (2018)
4. Bachman, P., Hjelm, R.D., Buchwalter, W.: Learning representations by maximizing mutual information across views. In: Advances in Neural Information Processing Systems, vol. 32 (2019)
5. Bateni, P., Barber, J., van de Meent, J.W., Wood, F.: Enhancing few-shot image classification with unlabelled examples. In: Proceedings of the IEEE/CVF Winter Conference on Applications of Computer Vision, pp. 2796–2805 (2022)
6. Boudiaf, M., Ziko, I., Rony, J., Dolz, J., Piantanida, P., Ben Ayed, I.: Information maximization for few-shot learning. In: Advances in Neural Information Processing Systems, vol. 33, pp. 2445–2457 (2020)
7. Bronskill, J., Gordon, J., Requeima, J., Nowozin, S., Turner, R.: TaskNorm: rethinking batch normalization for meta-learning. In: International Conference on Machine Learning, pp. 1153–1164. PMLR (2020)
8. Caron, M., Bojanowski, P., Joulin, A., Douze, M.: Deep clustering for unsupervised learning of visual features. In: Proceedings of the European Conference on Computer Vision (ECCV), pp. 132–149 (2018)
9. Caron, M., Bojanowski, P., Mairal, J., Joulin, A.: Unsupervised pre-training of image features on non-curated data. In: Proceedings of the IEEE/CVF International Conference on Computer Vision, pp. 2959–2968 (2019)
10. Chen, T., Kornblith, S., Norouzi, M., Hinton, G.: A simple framework for contrastive learning of visual representations. In: International Conference on Machine Learning, pp. 1597–1607. PMLR (2020)
11. Chen, W.Y., Liu, Y.C., Kira, Z., Wang, Y.C.F., Huang, J.B.: A closer look at few-shot classification. In: International Conference on Learning Representations (2018)
12. Chen, Z., Ge, J., Zhan, H., Huang, S., Wang, D.: Pareto self-supervised training for few-shot learning. In: Proceedings of the IEEE/CVF Conference on Computer Vision and Pattern Recognition, pp. 13663–13672 (2021)
13. Chen, Z., Maji, S., Learned-Miller, E.: Shot in the dark: few-shot learning with no base-class labels. In: Proceedings of the IEEE/CVF Conference on Computer Vision and Pattern Recognition, pp. 2668–2677 (2021)
14. Co-Reyes, J.D., et al.: Meta-learning language-guided policy learning. In: International Conference on Learning Representations, vol. 3 (2019)
15. Craig, J.J.: Introduction to Robotics: Mechanics and Control. Pearson Educacion (2005)
16. Deng, J., Dong, W., Socher, R., Li, L.J., Li, K., Fei-Fei, L.: ImageNet: a large-scale hierarchical image database. In: 2009 IEEE Conference on Computer Vision and Pattern Recognition, pp. 248–255. IEEE (2009)
17. Dhillon, G.S., Chaudhari, P., Ravichandran, A., Soatto, S.: A baseline for few-shot image classification. In: International Conference on Learning Representations (2019)
18. Doersch, C., Gupta, A., Zisserman, A.: Crosstransformers: spatially-aware few-shot transfer. In: Advances in Neural Information Processing Systems, vol. 33, pp. 21981–21993 (2020)

19. Fei-Fei, L., Fergus, R., Perona, P.: One-shot learning of object categories. IEEE Trans. Pattern Anal. Mach. Intell. **28**(4), 594–611 (2006)
20. Fink, M.: Object classification from a single example utilizing class relevance metrics. In: Advances in Neural Information Processing Systems, vol. 17 (2004)
21. Finn, C., Abbeel, P., Levine, S.: Model-agnostic meta-learning for fast adaptation of deep networks. In: International Conference on Machine Learning, pp. 1126–1135. PMLR (2017)
22. Garcia, V., Bruna, J.: Few-shot learning with graph neural networks. arXiv preprint arXiv:1711.04043 (2017)
23. Gidaris, S., Bursuc, A., Komodakis, N., Pérez, P., Cord, M.: Boosting few-shot visual learning with self-supervision. In: Proceedings of the IEEE/CVF International Conference on Computer Vision, pp. 8059–8068 (2019)
24. Gidaris, S., Singh, P., Komodakis, N.: Unsupervised representation learning by predicting image rotations. In: International Conference on Learning Representations (2018)
25. Goodfellow, I., et al.: Generative adversarial networks. Commun. ACM **63**(11), 139–144 (2020)
26. Gutstein, S., Fuentes, O., Freudenthal, E.: Knowledge transfer in deep convolutional neural nets. Int. J. Artif. Intell. Tools **17**(03), 555–567 (2008)
27. Hadsell, R., Chopra, S., LeCun, Y.: Dimensionality reduction by learning an invariant mapping. In: 2006 IEEE Computer Society Conference on Computer Vision and Pattern Recognition (CVPR 2006), vol. 2, pp. 1735–1742. IEEE (2006)
28. He, K., Fan, H., Wu, Y., Xie, S., Girshick, R.: Momentum contrast for unsupervised visual representation learning. In: Proceedings of the IEEE/CVF Conference on Computer Vision and Pattern Recognition, pp. 9729–9738 (2020)
29. He, K., Zhang, X., Ren, S., Sun, J.: Deep residual learning for image recognition. In: Proceedings of the IEEE Conference on Computer Vision and Pattern Recognition (CVPR) (2016)
30. Hong, Y., Niu, L., Zhang, J., Zhang, L.: Matchinggan: matching-based few-shot image generation. In: 2020 IEEE International Conference on Multimedia and Expo (ICME), pp. 1–6. IEEE (2020)
31. Hu, S.X., Li, D., Stühmer, J., Kim, M., Hospedales, T.M.: Pushing the limits of simple pipelines for few-shot learning: external data and fine-tuning make a difference. In: Proceedings of the IEEE/CVF Conference on Computer Vision and Pattern Recognition, pp. 9068–9077 (2022)
32. Jha, S., Seshia, S.A.: A theory of formal synthesis via inductive learning. Acta Inform. **54**(7), 693–726 (2017). https://doi.org/10.1007/s00236-017-0294-5
33. Jing, L., Tian, Y.: Self-supervised visual feature learning with deep neural networks: a survey. IEEE Trans. Pattern Anal. Mach. Intell. **43**(11), 4037–4058 (2020)
34. Kim, J., Kim, T., Kim, S., Yoo, C.D.: Edge-labeling graph neural network for few-shot learning. In: Proceedings of the IEEE/CVF Conference on Computer Vision and Pattern Recognition, pp. 11–20 (2019)
35. Lake, B.M., Salakhutdinov, R., Tenenbaum, J.B.: Human-level concept learning through probabilistic program induction. Science **350**(6266), 1332–1338 (2015)
36. Ledig, C., et al.: Photo-realistic single image super-resolution using a generative adversarial network. In: Proceedings of the IEEE Conference on Computer Vision and Pattern Recognition, pp. 4681–4690 (2017)
37. Liu, C., et al.: Learning a few-shot embedding model with contrastive learning. In: AAAI (2021)
38. Liu, Y., et al.: Learning to propagate labels: transductive propagation network for few-shot learning. In: International Conference on Learning Representations (2018)

39. Luo, X., Chen, Y., Wen, L., Pan, L., Xu, Z.: Boosting few-shot classification with view-learnable contrastive learning. In: 2021 IEEE International Conference on Multimedia and Expo (ICME), pp. 1–6. IEEE (2021)

40. Ma, J., Xie, H., Han, G., Chang, S.F., Galstyan, A., Abd-Almageed, W.: Partner-assisted learning for few-shot image classification. In: Proceedings of the IEEE/CVF International Conference on Computer Vision, pp. 10573–10582 (2021)

41. Mishra, N., Rohaninejad, M., Chen, X., Abbeel, P.: A simple neural attentive meta-learner. In: International Conference on Learning Representations (2018)

42. Nichol, A., Schulman, J.: Reptile: a scalable metalearning algorithm. arXiv preprint arXiv:1803.02999 2(3), 4 (2018)

43. Noroozi, M., Favaro, P.: Unsupervised learning of visual representations by solving jigsaw puzzles. In: Leibe, B., Matas, J., Sebe, N., Welling, M. (eds.) ECCV 2016. LNCS, vol. 9910, pp. 69–84. Springer, Cham (2016). https://doi.org/10.1007/978-3-319-46466-4_5

44. Oreshkin, B., Rodríguez López, P., Lacoste, A.: Tadam: task dependent adaptive metric for improved few-shot learning. In: Advances in Neural Information Processing Systems, vol. 31 (2018)

45. Ouali, Y., Hudelot, C., Tami, M.: Spatial contrastive learning for few-shot classification. In: Oliver, N., Pérez-Cruz, F., Kramer, S., Read, J., Lozano, J.A. (eds.) ECML PKDD 2021. LNCS (LNAI), vol. 12975, pp. 671–686. Springer, Cham (2021). https://doi.org/10.1007/078-3-030-80486-6_41

46. Pathak, D., Krahenbuhl, P., Donahue, J., Darrell, T., Efros, A.A.: Context encoders: feature learning by inpainting. In: Proceedings of the IEEE Conference on Computer Vision and Pattern Recognition, pp. 2536–2544 (2016)

47. Pavan Kumar, M., Jayagopal, P.: Multi-class imbalanced image classification using conditioned GANs. Int. J. Multimedia Inf. Retrieval 10(3), 143–153 (2021)

48. Ren, M., et al.: Meta-learning for semi-supervised few-shot classification. In: International Conference on Learning Representations (2018)

49. Rodríguez, P., Laradji, I., Drouin, A., Lacoste, A.: Embedding propagation: smoother manifold for few-shot classification. In: Vedaldi, A., Bischof, H., Brox, T., Frahm, J.-M. (eds.) ECCV 2020. LNCS, vol. 12371, pp. 121–138. Springer, Cham (2020). https://doi.org/10.1007/978-3-030-58574-7_8

50. Royle, J.A., Dorazio, R.M., Link, W.A.: Analysis of multinomial models with unknown index using data augmentation. J. Comput. Graph. Stat. 16(1), 67–85 (2007)

51. Su, J.-C., Maji, S., Hariharan, B.: When does self-supervision improve few-shot learning? In: Vedaldi, A., Bischof, H., Brox, T., Frahm, J.-M. (eds.) ECCV 2020. LNCS, vol. 12352, pp. 645–666. Springer, Cham (2020). https://doi.org/10.1007/978-3-030-58571-6_38

52. Tang, X., Teng, Z., Zhang, B., Fan, J.: Self-supervised network evolution for few-shot classification. In: IJCAI, pp. 3045–3051 (2021)

53. Thrun, S., Pratt, L.: Learning to learn: Introduction and overview. In: Thrun, S., Pratt, L. (eds.) Learning to learn, pp. 3–17. Springer, Cham (1998). https://doi.org/10.1007/978-1-4615-5529-2_1

54. Tian, Y., Krishnan, D., Isola, P.: Contrastive multiview coding. In: Vedaldi, A., Bischof, H., Brox, T., Frahm, J.-M. (eds.) ECCV 2020. LNCS, vol. 12356, pp. 776–794. Springer, Cham (2020). https://doi.org/10.1007/978-3-030-58621-8_45

55. Tian, Y., Wang, Y., Krishnan, D., Tenenbaum, J.B., Isola, P.: Rethinking few-shot image classification: a good embedding is all you need? In: Vedaldi, A., Bischof, H., Brox, T., Frahm, J.-M. (eds.) ECCV 2020. LNCS, vol. 12359, pp. 266–282. Springer, Cham (2020). https://doi.org/10.1007/978-3-030-58568-6_16

56. Vilalta, R., Drissi, Y.: A perspective view and survey of meta-learning. Artif. Intell. Rev. **18**(2), 77–95 (2002)
57. Vinyals, O., Blundell, C., Lillicrap, T., Wierstra, D., et al.: Matching networks for one shot learning. In: Advances in Neural Information Processing Systems, vol. 29 (2016)
58. Wang, Y., Yao, Q., Kwok, J.T., Ni, L.M.: Generalizing from a few examples: a survey on few-shot learning. ACM Comput. Surv. (CSUR) **53**(3), 1–34 (2020)
59. Wei, C., et al.: Iterative reorganization with weak spatial constraints: solving arbitrary jigsaw puzzles for unsupervised representation learning. In: Proceedings of the IEEE/CVF Conference on Computer Vision and Pattern Recognition, pp. 1910–1919 (2019)
60. Wu, Z., Xiong, Y., Yu, S.X., Lin, D.: Unsupervised feature learning via nonparametric instance discrimination. In: Proceedings of the IEEE Conference on Computer Vision and Pattern Recognition, pp. 3733–3742 (2018)
61. Yan, W., Yap, J., Mori, G.: Multi-task transfer methods to improve one-shot learning for multimedia event detection. In: BMVC, pp. 37–1 (2015)
62. Yang, L., Li, L., Zhang, Z., Zhou, X., Zhou, E., Liu, Y.: DPGN: distribution propagation graph network for few-shot learning. In: Proceedings of the IEEE/CVF Conference on Computer Vision and Pattern Recognition, pp. 13390–13399 (2020)
63. Yang, Z., Wang, J., Zhu, Y.: Few-shot classification with contrastive learning. arXiv preprint arXiv:2209.08224 (2022)
64. Ye, H.J., Hu, H., Zhan, D.C., Sha, F.: Few-shot learning via embedding adaptation with set-to-set functions. In: Proceedings of the IEEE/CVF Conference on Computer Vision and Pattern Recognition, pp. 8808–8817 (2020)
65. Zhang, C., Cai, Y., Lin, G., Shen, C.: DeepEMD: differentiable earth mover's distance for few-shot learning. arXiv preprint arXiv:2003.06777 (2020)
66. Zhang, R., Isola, P., Efros, A.A.: Colorful image colorization. In: Leibe, B., Matas, J., Sebe, N., Welling, M. (eds.) ECCV 2016. LNCS, vol. 9907, pp. 649–666. Springer, Cham (2016). https://doi.org/10.1007/978-3-319-46487-9_40
67. Zhang, Y., Yang, W., Sun, W., Ye, K., Chen, M., Xu, C.-Z.: The constrained GAN with hybrid encoding in predicting financial behavior. In: Wang, D., Zhang, L.-J. (eds.) AIMS 2019. LNCS, vol. 11516, pp. 13–27. Springer, Cham (2019). https://doi.org/10.1007/978-3-030-23367-9_2
68. Zhuang, F., Ren, L., Dong, Q., Sinnott, R.O.: A mobile application using deep learning to automatically classify adult-only images. In: Xu, R., De, W., Zhong, W., Tian, L., Bai, Y., Zhang, L.-J. (eds.) AIMS 2020. LNCS, vol. 12401, pp. 140–155. Springer, Cham (2020). https://doi.org/10.1007/978-3-030-59605-7_11

New Commonsense Views Inspired by Infants and Its Implications for Artificial Intelligence

Kai Liu[1,2], Ao-nan Wang[1,2], Nan Li[1,2(✉)], Han-lin Ma[3], and Hong-li Gao[4]

[1] School of Educational Sciences, Bohai University, Jinzhou 121013, China
ccnulk@ccnu.edu.cn
[2] Institute of Artificial General Intelligence, Bohai University, Jinzhou 121013, China
[3] School of Marxism, Suzhou University of Science and Technology, Suzhou 215009, China
[4] School of Psychology, Xinxiang Medical University, Xinxiang 453003, China

Abstract. Commonsense has long been a question of great interest in a wide range of disciplines but there has been little agreements on it. The research to date has tended to focus on commonsense with disciplinary characteristics rather than commonsense research itself. However, commonsense issues are inherently generic in nature and need to be considered from a broader perspective. It is the more effective way to investigate infants with generic characteristics in order to clarify the essence of commonsense. A new framework for a commonsense view of epistemic turnaround inspired by infant learning. It points out that commonsense not only has the characteristics of infant learning as embodiment, constructivity, and generativeness, but also has the characteristics of hierarchy of development, bounded relativity, embodiment of semantics, and axiomatic openness. In this paper, the term 'commonsense' will be used in its broadest sense to refer to a kind of useful background knowledge for an intelligent subject, and this background knowledge belongs to the adaptive experience actively constructed in the open environment. Finally, the enlightenment of this new commonsense view is discussed. In future research, it might be possible to be an opportunity to break the current limitations of Artificial Intelligence.

Keywords: Commonsense · Infant · Artificial intelligence · Characteristic · Definition

1 Introduction

At the scientific level, Commonsense is both a case of historical "unresolved" involving many disciplines and long-standing debates. It is also a realistic "bottleneck" that hinders the development of current artificial intelligence. The scientific myth of commonsense leads to the "dilemma" of knowledge engineering: On the one hand, a massive knowledge base with flexibility, low redundancy and reasoning can be used as support to improve the understanding level and application performance of smart devices. On the other hand, there is a growing awareness that common knowledge may not be exhaustive nor can it all be efficiently represented and processed. Moreover, instead of a positive gain between the expansion of the knowledge base and the increase in system intelligence, there is a

K. Ye and L.-J. Zhang (Eds.): CLOUD 2022, LNCS 13731, pp. 69–82, 2022.
https://doi.org/10.1007/978-3-031-23498-9_6

steep marginal benefit in terms of the storage and computational resource consumption of common knowledge.

Nowadays, it is urgent to reconsider the problem of commonsense from a scientific perspective. The emergence of general artificial intelligence systems that can think, have emotions, and have some level of self-awareness has broken the carbon-based boundaries of previous intelligent subjects and broadened the scope of commonsense research. The possibility of complementation and transfer of the "man-machine" dual knowledge not only highlights the importance and necessity of human commonsense exploration, but also reflects that commonsense is a necessary path to a deeper understanding of intelligence theory. Therefore, the combing, integration and innovative examination of commonsense research is both a breakthrough of the mainstream AI commonsense dilemma, an important development of cognitive science theory, and the first step towards the application practice of general AI systems.

2   Literature Review

2.1   Disciplinary Differences in Commonsense

Different Motivations: Disciplinary research motivations are the theoretical starting point for scientific cognition of commonsense. Philosophy is the oldest, most comprehensive, and most sufficient discipline to discuss commonsense. In order to measure the value of the discipline, traditional philosophy often takes the degree of deviation between itself and commonsense as a benchmark. In order to clarify the relationship between commonsense and philosophy, rationalists and empiricists make tit-for-tat on this issue [1]. In the field of computer science, commonsense is usually regarded as a technical problem to solve various commonsense problems from the application level. However, the commonsense problem is still a big obstacle to the development of artificial intelligence [2]. In order to make machines have more human-like thinking abilities, commonsense extraction and commonsense reasoning are becoming new research hotspots. In pedagogy, commonsense is usually studied as an application problem. From the perspective of axiology, educational position and commonsense are perfectly integrated. Commonsense that has not been decomposed in different forms of the education process can neither be deeply rooted in the hearts of people nor become a force to enlighten good humanity in the process of social operation. Education is to accumulate the outstanding ideas of the individual's experiences as commonsense which can be passed on through various forms of education [3]. Because different disciplines have different starting points and different perspectives and needs for commonsense, their views on commonsense are also different. They are often confined within the discipline and serve their own discipline as the main purpose, so it is difficult to generate motivation for cross field in-depth exploration.

Different Intensions: There is no unified understanding of the connotation of commonsense within the disciplines. In philosophy, some scholars regard commonsense as operational knowledge, which is a common cultural property based on everyone's similar understanding. Some scholars also screen commonsense from daily knowledge.

For example, Popper, the founder of critical rationalism, thinks that all science and philosophy are commonsense of civilization [4]. In computer science, researchers initially equated commonsense with expert knowledge. For example, some scholars compared commonsense to knowledge cloud based on the metaphor of the "atomic model" to obtain expert knowledge through knowledge cloud, while others compared commonsense to knowledge soup, which may contain many loosely coupled pieces, corresponding to typical frameworks, rules and facts in AI system [5]. In pedagogy, they hold two kinds of views. One is the commonsense in early childhood, for educational individuals, part of their commonsense comes from nature, and part of it comes from the valuable and universal content produced by the education system [3]. This kind of commonsense is used in the form of curriculum to improve the core quality of children in early childhood and help them understand the world and guide life; The other is general education, which correspondingly internalizes the gestalt integrating knowledge innovation and value norms in professional knowledge learning. It condenses into transferable metacognitive ability, meta ethical ability and meta appreciation ability, thus pointing to the goal of personality education in modern society [6]. This kind of commonsense tends to face higher education and is more professional and closed.

Different Functions: Functional understanding is the application foothold of scientific cognition of commonsense. In philosophy, Aristotle first proposed that commonsense is the ability to integrate materials obtained from the five special senses. Later, some scholars proposed that commonsense is an important means of human survival with stable predictability [7]. In the field of computer science, commonsense means being able to reason, learn and solve problems. The use of logical reasoning has made some progress in AI in the early days. But at present, most researchers choose another way to train neural networks with a large amount of data by deep learning and commonsense can make program learning more effective. In pedagogy, commonsense is always regarded as an innate ability, and people can use it to make wise and practical judgments without having to master special knowledge or receive special training [3]. Some scholars also put forward that commonsense is a rhetorical device, a conceptual tool, or a practical tool for transformation from an interdisciplinary perspective. Commonsense should be viewed as a cross-cultural variable [8].

2.2 Subject Consensus of Commonsense

Although differences of opinion still exist, there appears to be some agreement. From the perspective of different discipline characteristics, we can find three consensuses of commonsense.

Vagueness of Commonsense: Varies by Person. In the field of philosophy, it is difficult to define commonsense because of its natural fuzziness. Popper believes that the word "commonsense" is an extremely ambiguous term because it refers to an ambiguous and changeable thing [4]. In the field of computer science, it is believed that professional knowledge is generally accurate, and commonsense is people's intuitive understanding of the world, which has a lot of ambiguity. There is a gap of commonsense between human beings and computers and the expression of commonsense are uncertain. There can be great differences between the forms of knowledge that humans learn and that they use again [9]. Commonsense is difficult to ponder and closely related to the specific context. This kind of expression with individual or group characteristics cannot be recognized and obtained by computers. This fuzziness from nature to intuitive expression makes it difficult for commonsense to have a unified definition.

Relative Truth of Commonsense: Varies by Location. The content of commonsense isn't truth, it has spontaneous rationality. Moore said that commonsense is not derived from one or several so-called self assertion principles, and it is not an axiomatic theoretical system. The coordination between commonsense beliefs is based on people's life practice, rather than on the basic principles of a certain theory [10]. At present, the field of artificial intelligence is keen on the research of commonsense reasoning. Researchers have developed and revised commonsense logic systems, with no progress as a result. There are inconsistent and incompatible beliefs within commonsense, and most commonsense cannot be expressed. In a relatively closed and repeatedly communicating population, commonsense, as a local knowledge, is universal knowledge, with spontaneous legitimacy and rationality. However, this spontaneous rationality makes commonsense only meaningful to individuals or groups in the field, and this non truth makes it difficult for researchers who follow the logic of commonsense to promote research.

The Variability of Commonsense: Varies by Time. The changeability of commonsense is reflected in that it is a process of dynamic accumulation and continuation. Moore emphasized that commonsense will be in the process of development and change with life. Some thoughts that used to be considered as commonsense will no longer be considered. Chen Yajun argues that change is the ultimate destiny of commonsense. The stability of commonsense formed in history is relative, and commonsense must change, but the rate of change of different commonsense is quite different. Zhong Yixin, an expert in the field of artificial intelligence, proposed that knowledge is changeable, has its own ecological system, and the generation of commonsense knowledge needs to be accumulated and digested. Supported by the foundation of innate knowledge, with the input of external knowledge, knowledge gradually passes through "empirical knowledge" to "normative knowledge" and finally grows into commonsense knowledge [11]. Commonsense knowledge or ability is constantly accumulated and developed at the individual level and the group level. New experience may not play a substitute role, but to a certain extent, it continues to enable human beings to adapt to social life.

In a word, compared with the differences in commonsense, the consensus of all disciplines on commonsense is rare. Since the content of commonsense is mostly derived from the theory of knowledge, its core embodies vagueness, non-truth and fluidity, on which the consensus of various disciplines is mostly based. These three characteristics of consensus point out the problem of commonsense, answering the question of "what is not" of commonsense to a certain extent, but not giving the answer of "what is".

3 A New View of Commonsense Inspired by Infant Learning

There are many different opinions in various disciplines, and there is no definite conclusion in commonsense research. Explaining what commonsense is needs to be transformed in two ways. On the one hand, the above-mentioned disciplines have discussed commonsense from an objective perspective on a human unit. Returning to the problem itself, it should be shifted to a subjective perspective, in which the inquiry is conducted on an individual basis. On the other hand, previous researchers all took adults as the main research object, and the precondition was that adults had acquired different commonsense, so it was not pure enough to explore commonsense issues, which made the research object changed to infants. Because infants are born without commonsense, they are at the boundary of innate and acquired cognitive development, and the experience acquired in infancy can be more purely called commonsense, which does not involve professional knowledge at this time, which makes it possible to explore the "what" of commonsense more directly from the perspective of infants.

3.1 Commonsense Learning Characteristics of Infants

Embodiment: Human infants acquire initial commonsense in the form of embodiment. Just as early childhood interactions with the environment are accomplished through movement. Children develop their actions in the process of interaction with the environment and promote their cognitive development at the same time. The experience gained in the process of individual growth can be divided into two categories: predictable experience and conditional experience [12]. Expected experience is the experience that individuals of a species may obtain in the normal development process; Conditional experience depends on the specific environment of individual life and is unique to individuals. Among them, crawling is a common phenomenon in the development of human infants, which is a predictable experience, and the experience of infant crawling will promote children to obtain the permanence of objects. The emergence of object permanence is the bud of representation, and representation is an essential link in the formation of concepts. Therefore, embodied experience is the basic raw material for infants' commonsense. The initially acquired embodied general knowledge can facilitate the development of subsequent higher cognition, which gradually derives from the embodied stage to the abstract stage. This embodied commonsense experience is so essential that advanced cognition is based on it.

Generativeness: Infants' cognitive development is generative, with each stage building on the development of the previous stage's experience. For example, infants take the perceptual structure of objects and events in the visual world as the basis for representing knowledge, which is an important step towards the representation of classification ability or typical knowledge. The representation of knowledge must be based on the development of classification ability, otherwise every perceptual object that appears may be processed to produce endless information. For example, a large number of physical causal reasoning is developed according to the principle of all or nothing. The infant's initial representation grasped the essence of the problem (such as contact and noncontact), and then gradually developed the ability to more complex and accurately identify various changes related to the event results. Infants gradually develop from the understanding of the causal relationship of things to the understanding of the causes of actions of people and things. Therefore, infants can develop more complex cognitive abilities, which reflects the real motivation of infants to try to understand things and human behavior through the surface and perceptual phenomena. The abstract stage will form a more general high-level experience than the past experience. Commonsense at this stage will become more abstract at the next stage.

Constructivity: The commonsense learning of infants reflects the character of construction, in which a multi-path developmental approach to the process of constructing commonsense learning can be obtained by exploring the differences in the development of normal infants and blind infants. The joint attention of normal children depends on visual development. Although blind infants have no visual experience, they can also explain the attention position of objects and others depending on subtle and indirect clues. The delayed acquisition of joint attention by blind infants confirms the importance of vision for this development, and shows that vision is not necessary for the occurrence of common attention. Although blind infants cannot obtain experience information through visual channels, they can still obtain information through auditory and tactile channels, and finally develop this ability [13]. Infant commonsense is dynamically constructed, and experience is constantly accumulated and revised according to the environment. However, the revised experience can not be guaranteed to be completely correct, but the commonsense applicable to infants is derived and developed in the construction.

In conclusion, there are always embodied, generative and constructive in the process of infants' commonsense learning. Take the number concept of children as an example, a number is an object that cannot be perceived from the micro level. Number knowledge is the abstract relationship between numbers. This knowledge development initially relies on concrete things that mediate such abstract relations, thus infants need to develop perceptual experiences in this process. The development of the number concept of children requires four stages, namely, the operation of quantity, quantity and number, and the ability to obtain the operation of number, The first three stages of development and construction are needed before children can extract numbers from the relationship between quantities existing in objective objects for number operations. In this process, children's number development must start with perceptual experience and then construct conceptual entities, and the development of the latter stage is always based on the previous stage [14]. From the macro level, the construction of children's number concept is a gradual process, which can not be separated from specific life experience. Children gradually develop from counting behavior without special significance to thinking activity of actively constructing mathematical abstract relations. Research in the field of cognition shows that the same is true of early cognitive development. Individuality, constructiveness and generativity depend on each other. In the process of construction, we need embodied experience. Constructiveness mainly emphasizes the construction process of learning experience, while generativity emphasizes the nature of time and the characteristics of change. The three characteristics are intertwined in the process of infant knowledge learning.

3.2   A New View of Commonsense

The only consensus among disciplines on commonsense is not based on the question of commonsense itself, but mostly on Epistemology, which makes commonsense inevitably take on the character of "knowledge". However, due to the limitations of Epistemology itself, commonsense is usually embedded in this contextual framework of interpretation. The result is that most of these "consensuses" can only propose but not solve problems or are good at "breaking the old" rather than "making the new". There is a need for a broader perspective and a more general insight into commonsense inspired by infant learning. The general framework is as follows (see Fig. 1).

New Perspectives. Commonsense needs to be viewed from a generic perspective, breaking down the barriers between disciplines and thinking about this open field in terms of commonsense. The new view of commonsense elaborates the general law of the occurrence and development of commonsense from the macro level of Epistemology; and introduces the mechanism of commonsense from the micro-level by drawing on the strengths of cognitive science, forming a scientific commonsense understanding with a general nature and studying the whole open field, and its innovation is mainly reflected in the following three aspects:

Firstly, the perspective Shifts from Objective to Subjective. In terms of the subject of commonsense, its effective subject should be expanded to human, animal, and intelligent systems. The subject should also be more generic, extending the scope to intelligent life forms, where the form of life bearing does not determine everything, but the focus is on intelligence and having a perceptual system that can prepare for the derivative construction of experience. As far as the content of common knowledge is concerned, it is the experience that is meaningful to the subject that becomes commonsense. So, this paper proposes to turn to the individual level and discuss experiences that are meaningful to the subject to which they belong.

Secondly, the Focus Shifts from Indirect Experience to Direct Experience. The initial source of commonsense involves embodiment, and these embodied experiences give an individual's commonsense unique meaning, laying the foundation for the subsequent development of higher-order abstract experiences. For example, infants' movements can access external experiences and refine perceptions, based on which they can help cognitive restructuring and construction. Embodied experience can help individuals acquire commonsense experience from passive to active, gradually help them interact with the environment, expand the scope of interaction, and thus acquire more new experiences. The rich expansion of commonsense perception experience can promote the subsequent dynamic construction and the derivative development of commonsense.

Lastly, the Theoretical Focus Shifts from Emergent Generative Theory to Reductive Generative Theory. The Emergency Generative Theory regards the knowledge system as a self-organizing system. At the overall level, the generation of knowledge is manifested as an Emergent existence [15]. The process of emergence is a black box, and the process of knowledge emergence is unknowable. Therefore, such scholars equate "common knowledge" with objective knowledge of limited extension, which emerges over time. In

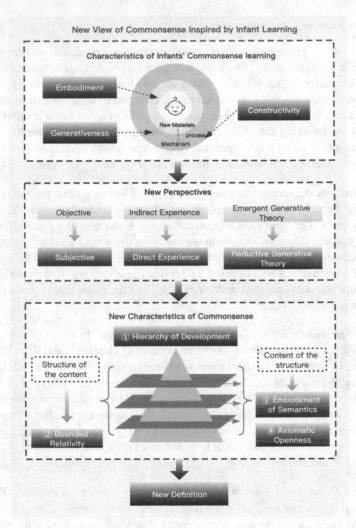

Fig. 1. The framework of new view of commonsense inspired by infant learning.

fact, there is a possibility that an important prerequisite for knowledge generation is based on an individual's past experience and that this experience is traceable. Different old experiences are constructed into new experiences that become new common knowledge that is meaningful to the individual. The mechanism of this construction is an innate common pattern, and the content is different experiences learned, and these create new commonsense through the construction. So the emergence of new commonsense tends to be understood as a traceable retrospective.

New Characteristics: The shift in perspective on commonsense provides a framework for exploring a new view of commonsense that derives four new features of commonsense from the three features of infant commonsense learning. The shift in perspective on commonsense provides a framework for exploring a new view of commonsense that derives four new features of commonsense from the three features of infant commonsense learning. Hierarchy is the result of the infant's commonsense learning, which starts from the structure of its features and gets the remaining three features. On the one hand, the structure of the content is explored to get the characteristic of bounded relativity; on the other hand, the content of the structure is sought to get the characteristic of semantic embodiment and openness without truth.

Hierarchy of Development: The derivative development of commonsense is crucial, which is not the same as the simple accumulation of acquired experience, but a hierarchical development through derivation. Initially acquiring perceptual raw material through embodiment, it operates using derivative mechanisms and continues to be constructed in the process, resulting in a hierarchical commonsense. It allows people to decide how to combine experiences efficiently within a limited time and limited resources to adapt to the current environment. The development of commonsense experience has a strict chronological order, and specialized knowledge cannot emerge without the foundation of generic knowledge. Specialized commonsense is based on general commonsense, just as a six-year-old child cannot understand the meaning of the universe without a general knowledge of physics and philosophy.

Bounded Relativity. The concept of "commonsense" needs to be viewed relatively, and this relativity is not infinite. The boundary lies between the direct experience acquired by the individual after birth (absolute commonsense) to the boundary of relative commonsense. There is no absolute commonsense beyond that, only adaptive commonsense for the situation at hand. Many scholars look at commonsense in layers, with Smith dividing it into three levels, with the bottom level being the world of commonsense, the middle level being cognitive activity, and the top level being pre-scientific beliefs [16]. Chen Yajun believes that the world of commonsense is based on information from the world, and on top of that, basic knowledge in various fields is the premise of cognition and common values in life are the premise of action. The two views contradict each other; the former believe that the world of commonsense is objective and does not depend on human cognitive activity; the latter believes that the human world is embodied through commonsense and that the world of commonsense and human cognition are mutually embedded. In fact, both do not clarify the premise of commonsense, which is the relativity of boundedness. The world of commonsense that Smith refers to is objectively unique, and this absoluteness denies that commonsense exists because it has meaning for individuals. Another view does not mention the existence of absolute commonsense, but the direct experience acquired during infancy should be absolute commonsense, which is the basis of human existence and relative commonsense as well. On the other hand, in terms of truth characteristics, commonsense is not absolutely correct, and new commonsense may challenge the existence of old commonsense and give new meaning to the subject. It is clear from the above that commonsense should not be considered at this level. Neither absolute nor infinite relativity, the relative indirect commonsense experience is since based on the absolute direct commonsense experience, which is expressed as stage relative commonsense and intruth relative commonsense.

Embodiment of Semantics: Before making a judgment in the open world, understand the contents of commonsense through embodiment and have an object of judgment.

The semantic symbols understood by the individual are supported by the embodied experience of perceptual-motor integration, and reality-cognition-language is a process in which the individual's initiative is generated by interaction with the outside world [17]. Two principles of the meaning of commonsense experience are derived here. One is the principle of relativity of empirical meaning - meaning is given to each other, and subjects can give meaning to each other when they acquire various kinds of information in the world of commonsense. For example, children cannot understand numbers at first, so the meaning of numbers is illustrated by the number of physical objects, like one or two pieces of candy, one or two trees, and these experiences. Another is the principle of the growth of the meaning of experience - the growth of the combination of meaning. In the process of constructing commonsense experiences, if there are two experiences A and B, only AB can be produced, but when C is added, there can be AC, BC and ABC. And so on, the meaning between commonsense experiences develops in combinatorial growth [18]. The individual's pre-experience gives meaning with subjective characteristic semantics, but this does not affect the individual's communication in the open world.

Axiomatic Openness: IN the open real world, the acquired commonsense is based on bounded relativity, which is not commonsense in the absolute sense, and the premise where common knowledge is established needs to be considered in context. There is a contradiction in commonsense in the open world, and this contradiction manifests itself as a paradox. Paradoxes have two types of conflict manifestations, one is the nature of internal conflict in the same world (self-contradiction), which is an irreconcilable contradiction at the same level, and the other is the nature of the conflict between what is essentially the same world but actually different worlds. This contradiction makes even the already constructed experiences changeable. Generally speaking, the old experience should be in the inner layer and the new experience in the outer layer, but in fact, the new experience may enter the inner layer by way of constructs to shake up the underlying experience. Both correct and incorrect constructs are about the choice of material for experience, and both are equally an adaptation to the current situation. Even if the constructs are wrong, "commonsense" is still reasonable for the individual and can be adapted to the present.

New Definition: The development of commonsense learning in human infants has laid the foundation for the search of commonsense fundamentals. Numerous studies have demonstrated the existence of the term "commonsense", but its existence needs to be considered in what sense it exists. Commonsense exists on the premise of adaptability, which is reflected in the ability of human beings to adapt to the open world of commonsense. The commonsense information available is limited and may conflict with old experiences, but it is still possible to respond to unlimited needs with limited resources and to respond to future possibilities with past experiences [19]. However, all these commonsense experiences need to be meaningful to the subject in the present moment in order to become individual commonsense. Therefore, there is no common knowledge in the absolute sense, only in the relative sense. This relative generality determines that its comprehensible common knowledge is useful background knowledge for intelligent subjects (humans, animals, machines), which belongs to the adaptive experience actively constructed for the open environment.

4   The Inspiration of the New View of Commonsense to AI

The generic character of commonsense issues dictates that the problem should be viewed from a holistic perspective. Nowadays, AI is a comprehensive discipline with computer, philosophy, and psychology as its core, supplemented by brain neuroscience, information engineering, mathematics, etc. AI is also a typical discipline encompassing theory, technology, engineering, and application to ethics, which fits well with the research completeness of the commonsense problem itself. The problem of commonsense impedes the central task of AI development. In this way, AI research is a perspective that makes it easier to proceed from theoretical issues to the empirical landing of commonsense problems.

4.1   Commonsense Acquisition and Representation

The first problem is the difficulty of commonsense extraction. The vagueness, relative truth, and variability of commonsense determine the difficulty of judging what is commonsense. Machine learning can extract commonsense knowledge, but characteristically, there are three problems. Firstly, the process itself has no commonsense, what is carried out is the process of learning data and then solving the problem. Machines are not confronted with mere data, but with the world of commonsense. The process of machine learning itself does not possess commonsense when first confronted with the commonsense physical world. Secondly, poor recognition of commonsense. Some of the "common knowledge" acquired by the machine is different from that acquired by human beings, but it is only the symbols and programs that have been entered and the meanings they represent that have been set in place. Thirdly, the machine cannot understand all the information it recognizes. The information it can recognize is also based on symbols that can be expressed in language, but there is more implicit knowledge that is difficult to capture in language, let alone for the machine to understand these concepts.

The second problem is commonsense is difficult to characterize. Due to the lack of embodied experience based on perceptual experience, all models of artificial intelligence constructed by the symbolist agenda follow the form of logical operations. In addition to the formal symbol system, it is impossible to construct another symbol system compatible with it, and commonsense knowledge cannot be formally represented [20]. But it is precisely through these perceptual experiences that humans construct their own knowledge systems. For example, when learning to swim, it is easy to search for a textual representation of the experience, but some people still cannot learn it because of the involvement of embodied experience. This experiential perceptual experience may be integrated in a more abstract way behind other experiences.

The last problem is small data makes it difficult to accomplish big tasks. Enda Wu said the next direction of AI is to move from big data to small data. But there is a huge gulf at every step from the extraction of to its representation. Commonsense is essentially a relative category of knowledge, which is always extended by a more basic subset and has a distinctly subjective empirical dimension. Therefore, there is no clear boundary of how "small" small data is. This is not a technical problem, but a theoretical problem. Commonsense acquisition and representation are successfully solved, but the amount of data is not enough to train a model that can solve the common knowledge problem.

The above commonsense problems encountered in the field of AI cannot be fundamentally solved because these dilemmas lie mainly in theory rather than technique [21].

4.2 Commonsense Organization and Reasoning

There are two main challenges at the individual level which are interpretability and combinatorial explosion. First is the issue of interpretability, although human-to-human interpretation is not completely interpretable, the model in deep learning is basically uninterpretable, which determines that interpretability is a matter of degree. There are already machines that perform commonsense reasoning with very high accuracy, for example, KDDI 2022 sets a new world record for commonsense reasoning with the ACROSS model. It still has not jumped out of the technical framework, which regards the human thinking process as knowledge inference and further expands the knowledge base and training volume, but the meaningless model parameters and high fit results in it do not show how the machine learns and uses commonsense. Back to the starting point of deep learning, the first way to try to achieve artificial intelligence is to use a simulation of the human brain and explain human intelligent activity through a network of neurons. It may seem that each step of the algorithm can be based on the source, but only at the computational level represents explainable. In fact, explainable needs to reproduce the process of commonsense organization reasoning, how to use commonsense, and solve the problem. The human network of commonsense experience is derived and constructed in such a way that individuals, when processing new information, choose to process only that which is valuable to them and store it according to its importance, enriching the network of empirical memory. It is because of the constructs based on the empirical meaning that individuals are able to consider well whether to process, organize or store, and to know why to process information in this way without redundancy and unexplainable work. But neural networks algorithms lack derivative and constructive processes, signal-oriented groups of neuronal networks do not make sense, and these models can only be unexplained.

The combinatorial explosion problem is a thorny problem in commonsense inference and organization. Deep neural networks have been on the rise since Alex Net performed well in the ImageNet competition, but at the same time, the limitations have become more pronounced. Deep learning always requires a large amount of annotated data, and the huge workload makes it easy for researchers to put the cart before the horse and focus on easy-to-follow tasks at the expense of the important ones. The finite size of the dataset makes neural networks overly sensitive to context, and to ensure that they can handle all problems would require infinitely large datasets that explore all possible spaces. The good performance of a neural network on a benchmark dataset does not mean that it will succeed in the real world. For this reason, mainstream artificial intelligence is constantly updated to develop algorithms that can cope with combinatorial explosions, such as the use of the combinatoriality principle. In the problem of testing combinatorial data, game theory chooses to focus on the worst case rather than the average case to solve the problem [22]. In fact, the primary reason why the combinatorial explosion problem can arise is that it is inevitable and unavoidable if considered only at the computational level. The openness of the commonsense world predicts the failure of the computational direction in the face of the inexhaustible commonsense information from the real world. And there is no combinatorial explosion problem for humans. From the experience level of the subject's perspective, for example, infants are able to apply broad knowledge successfully to specific challenges [23]. Although individuals can have many combinations of commonsense experiences, individuals choose only those combinations that are meaningful to them in the present. They make combinatorial inferences based on past experiences so that in the face of an open world of common knowledge, individuals are able to use common knowledge experiences efficiently reducing the circuit of combinatorial explosion.

References

1. Markie, P.: Rationalism vs. empiricism. In: Zalta, E.D. (eds.) Stanford Encyclopedia of Philosophy (fall 2008 edition). The Metaphysics Research Lab, Stanford (2008)
2. Piloto, L.S., et al.: Intuitive physics learning in a deep-learning model inspired by developmental psychology. Nat. Hum. Behav. 6(9), 1257–1267 (2022)
3. Wu, S.: Education and general knowledge. Thinking 33(1), 1–5 (2007)
4. Popper, K.R.: Objective Knowledge, vol. 360. Oxford University Press, Oxford (1972)
5. Sowa, J.F.: Crystallizing theories out of knowledge soup. Intell. Syst. State Art Future Direct. 456–487 (1990)
6. You, X.: The origin and current situation of contemporary Chinese general education: also on the significance of general education evaluation-adjustment mechanism. J. East China Norm. Univ. (Educ. Sci. Edn.) 40(8), 1 (2022)
7. Wartofsky, M.W.: Conceptual foundation of scientific thought an introduction to the philosophy of science (1968)
8. Torres, C.A.: The neoliberal common sense and global universities: knowledge commodification in higher education. Peking Univ. Educ. Rev. 12(1), 2–16 (2014)
9. McCarthy, J.: Programs with common sense. RLE and MIT Computation Center, Cambridge (1960)
10. Moore, G.E.: A defence of common sense. In: Philosophical Papers. George Allen & Unwin, London (1925)
11. Zhong, Y.: Breakthroughs in artificial intelligence and innovation in methodology. Pattern Recogn. Artif. Intell. 25(3), 456–461 (2012)
12. Greenough, W.T., Black, J.E., Wallace, C.S.: Experience and brain development. In: Johnson, M.H., Munakata, Y., Gilmore, R.O. (eds.) Brain Development and Cognition: A Reader, pp. 186–216. Blackwell Publishing (2002)
13. Bigelow, A.E.: The development of joint attention in blind infants. Dev. Psychopathol. 15(2), 259–275 (2003)
14. Zhou, X.: The Early Development of Children's Number Concept, pp. 43–45. East China Normal University Press, Shanghai (2004)
15. Li, X.: Knowledge System Theory. Science Press, Beijing (2011)
16. Smith, B.: Formal ontology, common sense and cognitive science. Int. J. Hum. Comput. Stud. 43(5–6), 641–667 (1995)
17. Merleau-Ponty, M.: Phenomenology of Perception. Routledge, London (1962). Transl. C Smith (From French)
18. Vasseleu, C.: Textures of Light: Vision and Touch in Irigaray, Levinas and Merleau Ponty. Routledge (2002)
19. Wang, P.: The assumptions on knowledge and resources in models of rationality. Int. J. Mach. Conscious. 3(01), 193–218 (2011)

20. Anderson, M.L.: Embodied cognition: a field guide. Artif. Intell. **149**(1), 91–130 (2003)
21. Wang, P.: On defining artificial intelligence. J. Artif. Gener. Intell. **10**(2), 1–37 (2019)
22. Yuille, A.L., Liu, C.: Deep nets: what have they ever done for vision? Int. J. Comput. Vision **129**(3), 781–802 (2021)
23. Monroe, D.: Seeking artificial common sense. Commun. ACM **63**(11), 14–16 (2020)

Analysis of Data Micro-governance in Full Life Cycle Management of the Leased Assets

Xiaofeng Gou[✉]

DAMA China, 76-78 Jiangchang San Lu, Suite 806, Jingan District, Shanghai, China
gouxff@126.com

Abstract. Combined with the characteristics of finance leasing industry in this thesis, matured technologies of the GIS satellite remote sensing and Internet of things are applied to the full life cycle management of leased assets. And combined with the theoretical knowledge framework of DAMA data management system, which making data management ideas and methods are practiced in the online asset management platform project. This study considerably provides some ideas and references to effectively tackle the hassle of the asset management, exploring data valuation and implementing the "micro governance" of data management system in the industry.

Keywords: Digital transformation · Internet of Things · Financial leasing · Asset management · Data management

1 Introduction

1.1 Background

According to the definition of the financial lease contract in the Civil Code of the People's Republic of China, the financial lease is a transaction act of Non bank financial composition form based on ownership transfer of enterprise or personal means of production Financial leasing is a transaction that "the lessor" purchases the lease item from the seller according to the lessee's choice of the seller and the lease item, provides it to the lessee for use, and the lessee pays the rent". It is clear that the lease item (hereinafter referred to as the "Leased Assets"), as a key element of the contract, belongs to the lessor (hereinafter referred to as the "Financial Lease Company"). If the lessee fails to normally carry out the lease, the financial leasing Company may recover and dispose of the leased assets in order to recover the funds. However, in the practice of financial leasing, when the lessee has malicious breach or fraud, the lessee may use the transaction rules of financial leasing to hide or transfer the leased assets in advance. Therefore, financial leasing companies need to timely understand and control the information of the ownership, value, operation and early warning of the leasing assets, in order to better serve the full life cycle and the whole process management of the leasing assets, and at the same time help to make more accurate evaluation and management of the key indicators like the lessee's operation, management and credit ability. So as to intervene in a timely manner at the initial stage of risk, and guarantee the financial leasing company to recover the financing principal to the greatest extent.

K. Ye and L.-J. Zhang (Eds.): CLOUD 2022, LNCS 13731, pp. 83–95, 2022.
https://doi.org/10.1007/978-3-031-23498-9_7

1.2 Pain Points

The essence of financial leasing is to take financing as the means and financing as the purpose. Financial leasing should focus on the value management, risk management and market management of leased assets. However, due to the development and evolution of the domestic financial leasing industry and its own characteristics, domestic financial leasing companies have formed credit financing businesses focusing on credit financing, commonly known as "quasi credit" financing businesses, based on enterprise operation and credit in the process of business development: financial leasing companies tend to pay more attention to the credit of the enterprise itself or the guarantee enterprise, or the effectiveness of credit enhancement measures. The market circulation value or asset management ability of non leased assets has brought certain challenges to the management of leased assets. The management pain points are mainly reflected in the following aspects:

Missing Basic Information. In the past, there was often a lack of attention to asset-base information collection, which led to the subsequent need to "retrofit" the management of leased assets to make up for short. However, the basic data collection of historical project assets is relatively difficult and costly. Moreover, the lessee's cooperation is not high, and the business personnel of financial leasing companies are not energetic enough, so the basic information and data of leased assets are often unable to be effectively collected and supplemented.

Complex Asset Types. According to the Interim Measures for the Supervision and Management of Financial Leasing Companies issued in 2020. In the current practice of financial leasing, there are generally two criteria for the selection of leased assets: (1) leased assets should be fixed assets; (2) The real right should be clear and can produce the right of income. Based on the above criteria, the selection range of leased assets is very wide, resulting in different asset information dimensions, and it is impossible to manage leased asset information with a unified general data template.

Customer Willingness is Not Strong. Since the management of leased assets is in the field of "post lease management" in traditional financial leasing, that is, the starting point of the management of leased assets is often after the contract is performed, and the lessee's financing purpose has been basically achieved at this time, the subsequent willingness to cooperate with the management of leased assets is not high, and frequent tracking of asset information may interfere with the lessee's production and operation activities, As a result, customer loyalty has declined in the highly competitive financial leasing market, and even customers with strong financing ability choose to replace financial leasing companies to conduct business.

High Control Cost. Before the introduction of scientific and technological means, the conventional management and control mode mainly used the on-site visits of asset managers of financial leasing companies to judge the existence and operation of leased assets. Such traditional means not only have shortcomings such as poor timeliness and easy fraud, but also consume relatively high time costs, capital costs and management costs for financial leasing companies when leasing assets are spread all over the country. For the sake of cost-effectiveness, finance leasing companies often give priority to customers with overdue records or high operating risks, which cannot be managed in a large scale, and it is difficult to achieve the goal of prevention and control in advance.

Value Needs Urgent Attention. For financial leasing companies, they often have the "right to dispose" of the leased assets according to the contract, and can dispose of the leased assets when the lessee defaults. At this time, if the ownership of the leased asset is clear, the market liquidity is good, and the disposal value is high, the remaining principal of the contract can be covered to resolve the risk; On the contrary, if the ownership of the leased asset cannot be clearly identified or the value is difficult to realize in the market, the financial loss cannot be recovered. Therefore, it is necessary to adopt effective means to continuously pay attention to value changes in the process of post lease management.

No Unified Standard in the Industry. Although domestic financial leasing industry has entered the development stage of leapfrog back to the origin, the relevant regulation and legislation is still in the process of improving and perfecting. Plus there are differences in practice, standards and regulations between types of financial lease companies, the industry has yet no relatively detailed management standards, and lacks of motivation for the regulation of leasing assets management.

1.3 Purpose and Meaning

The establishment of a sound management ability of leasing assets enables the effective tracking on operation of the lessee and the prompt intervene before the change, loss and damage of the leased assets so that the leasing property can play a role of risk release. Management and utilization of the data of the leased assets can provide a decision basis for the strategic analysis of the capital investment planning and reduce the management cost and management scope of the post-leasing asset management personnel, which is a very meaningful digital transformation practice of the financial leasing industry [1].

With the increasing matured technology of the Internet of Things and satellite remote sensing, this study goes deeply in architecture design of the online management platform for leasing assets and in the application of data management system, which not only helps to solve the business difficulties, but also has important practical significance in implementation of the data management system in the financial leasing industry, the Internet of things, and the asset management.

1.4 Achievements

According to the characteristics of the financial leasing industry, this application and research constructs an available online management platform for leasing assets and puts forward a data management system and scheme based on the above architecture. The implementation and operation of the platform reflect the business value of the online management platform for leased assets, which has a good inspiration and demonstration significance for the data management system to play a positive role in the business and digital transformation field.

2   Management Requirements Analysis and Platform Solutions

2.1   Management Needs of Financial Leased Assets

The essence of a leased asset is a "thing". Leased assets cannot be managed as conventional assets due to the facts that they have the dual role of "credit enhancement" and "risk slow release" in financial leasing transactions. The routine registration of leased assets can only form a good protection in the ownership identification of assets, but there are still great deficiencies and gaps in the value, status and risk management of the leased assets. With the continuation of the strict supervision situation of financial leasing companies, the real and effective management of "things" should be achieved, whether for the consideration of their own operation or in response to the regulatory requirements of relevant financial management departments.

2.2   Related Technologies

Satellite Remote Sensing Technology. Satellite remote sensing is a comprehensive science and technology, which mainly refers to the modern technology system that uses visible light, infrared, microwave and other detection instruments to photograph or scan, to induce, to transmit and to process information, so as to identify the nature and motion state of surface substances.

Base Station Positioning Technology. Mobile devices communicate in the mobile operator network through data (voice data, text data, multimedia data, etc.) through a cellular base station connected to the network. Base station positioning is to obtain the location information (latitude and longitude coordinates) of the mobile terminal users through these cellular base stations.

QR Code Technology. Since the 20th century, QR code has been widely used in various fields with its advantages of low cost, large storage capacity and fast identification speed. And the current popular one is QR code.

Current Sensor Technology. By contrast, the current sensor based on the loop ampere law, after decades of development, is mature in technology, suitable for batch production, reasonable in price, and widely used to meet the needs of the industrial field.

2.3   Construction Objectives of the Management Platform

In order to actively respond to the construction of digital economy and the construction of digital China, digital will be effectively introduced into the financial leasing scene, and to explore the field of post-lease asset management enabled by technology. The core idea of the leased asset management platform based on GIS and the Internet of Things discussed in this paper is to build an online life cycle management platform based on Taichung and micro-front-end architecture, to provide management and control ability for the leasing asset management of financial leasing companies, and to realize the overall goal of controllable, dynamically controllable and abnormal assets.

2.4 Brief Description of the Management Platform Architecture Design

The overall design scheme of the platform includes IoT acquisition layer, data fusion layer, middle platform application layer and application enabling layer.

IOT acquisition layer: Based on data interface, IoT communication, data persistence and other components, it is responsible for receiving, processing, forwarding and other message communication between the platform and IoT devices.

Data fusion layer: as the main force point of data governance, it is used to connect and integrate the basic data between the platform and other business systems and management systems and collect the asset management characteristic indicators according to the actual business, so as to realize the storage, association and fusion between the data fields.

Middle platform application layer: mainly responsible for providing basic service capabilities for the application enabling layer. Based on the demand-based application scenarios, the common business, technology, logic are abstract, packaged, precipitated and extracted into general modules to avoid the disadvantages of repeated construction between applications.

Application enabling layer: It mainly provides the company's management, professional management departments, relevant business managers and other service objects with front desk interactive support based on decision-making, management, early warning and other needs to meet the application needs of objects of different orientations and levels.

3 Micro-governance in Platform Construction

3.1 The Concept and Significance of Micro-governance

Micro governance can be understood as micro governance to achieve effective ground data governance system, work scope is not just governance framework and data culture, but more "data translator" in enterprises and organizations, detailed governance plans according to the characteristics of different data domain, and specific implementation for the strong targets.

3.2 Analysis of Data Characteristics and Management Difficulties of Leased Assets

Covering the Full Life Cycle of the Assets. The life cycle of the leased asset includes the process of generation, existence, operation, loss, loss (disposal) and so on, and its market value and depreciation value are gradually losing. For a financial leasing company, the management data shall run through the whole life cycle of the asset, from recording the relevant information of the lease assets to tracking the existence until the completion or loss or disposal of the lease contract.

Contains Multi-angle and Diversified Information Dimensions. Information dimension of leasing assets itself is relatively complex. Asset ownership information contains invoice information, basic information, related licenses and impact information, etc., while information reflecting asset operation situation has extremely rich unstructured data types (such as current, positioning, or video recording, etc.) according to different management means. Even when the asset capacity generates actual benefits, it is necessary to include the relevant information of its benefits into management monitoring, which poses new challenges to the storage and utilization of data.

"Storyline" Running from Assets to Business. According to previous discussions, asset management drives compliance and risk control. The asset management of the financial leasing business is still essentially based on risk prevention and control. When planning the data management, full consideration should be given to the business background of the financial leasing industry. It is very necessary to associate assets with their business context to perform association analysis and monitor when managing the assets.

With Complex Information Granularity. In the practical operation of the financial leasing industry, the number of leased assets will vary greatly according to the complexity of the business. It is necessary to abstract and summarize the data granularity and management needs of different financial leasing companies, and extensive management of "one size fits all" should not be used.

The Data Showed a Discrete Distribution. Because the information distribution of leased assets is scattered and complex, it is difficult to obtain, to save and to finance the data. For example, the registration information of leasing property in existing businesses needs to be obtained from the Internet, and the invoice and other information is obtained according to the asset type, and some data rely on business personnel to obtain paper materials offline. Some new rental items have their own Internet of Things attributes, such as new energy equipment, commercial vehicles, etc. However, these data are often distributed in the systems built by different suppliers, with different construction standards and deployment methods, which add difficulties to the realization of the online management platform for leased assets.

3.3 Requirement Analysis of the Leased Assets Data Service

After summarizing the data characteristics and difficulties of "things", facing these problems that need to be solved urgently, it is necessary to establish practical principles for leasing asset data management, which should be based on the data application requirements for asset management. After sufficient research and demonstration, the management needs of leased assets in the context of digital transformation are summarized as follows:

Substantial Management Based on Ownership. First of all, you need to record the basic information of the leased asset and relate it to the business context with the logic of blood tracing, for example, from the leased asset to the business development, due diligence control, contract performance and other lease business processes.

Value-Based Dynamic Tracking. The liquidity of the leased assets in the trading market should be fully considered. The value tracking of assets is not only conducive to asset disposal, but also conducive to financial leasing companies to guide and carry out financial leasing business.

Control Grasp Based on Operation. The operation and control of leased assets focuses on two aspects. One is the security of the assets, whether there are changes, transfer, damage; the other is the income of the leased assets, whose operation data can not only be calculated to predict the income of the assets according to the industry background and data intelligence, but also to predict whether the operation of the enterprise is good when the assets form a certain scale.

Continuous Early Warning Based on Risk. With continuous management and precipitation of data about ownership, value, operation data, it is required to further put forward the exploration of the early warning model based on risk. Through the data processing with risk factors, and free combination of dimensions such as enterprise characteristics and business classification, intelligent risk early warning module is formed to help financial risk prevention from the asset management perspective.

3.4 Practice of Micro-governance in the Online Management Platform of Leased Assets

Positioning and Correlation of Micro-governance and Data Architecture. As the landing methodology of the executive layer, data micro governance needs to be built on the organizational level data architecture. The composition of the architecture generally includes the organizational structure, specifications and common architecture tools of the architecture category according to the definition of the DAMA Management Association. As the guarantee of micro governance, it is necessary to actively understand the existing framework components of the organization when landing at the platform level, and undertake the guiding ideology, tools and processes of data architecture; Timely review in the whole process of platform implementation and micro governance, and continuously supplement and improve the data architecture to form a virtuous cycle.

Data Acquisition and Preprocessing. ETL technology is often used in data warehouses or data platforms, its role is to collect internal and external, multi-sources of data. In this case, it is more important to process the data of things such as satellite and Internet of Things [5].

Acquisition and Preprocessing Internet of Things. Data acquisition of The Internet of Things is to obtain the data from the terminal IOT sensors, and to transmits the data to the Logic layer through a unified data analysis protocol. The Logic layer is responsible for the analysis, aggregation, and finally persistence to the database. If there is a real-time push, the incoming message queue can meet the real-time communication scenario.

Space Satellite Map Acquisition and Preprocessing. Space satellite data collection uses manpower and AI for step by step processing, with the current relatively mature GIS processing program and space database for processing, the image is transformed into structured data available for analysis.

Internal and External System Data Collection and Preprocessing. The value, operation and early warning data of assets are mostly structured data, which is less difficult to analyze than the Internet of Things and aerospace data. However, because their data are distributed in multiple internal and external data sources, including financial leasing core business system, ownership registration related websites, second-hand trading market websites, partner information systems, etc. It is necessary to combine data modeling and way of distribution fusion to steadily promote the solution.

Design and Consideration of the Synchronization Mechanism. In this project case, the segmentation of the application scenarios will have different requirements according to the requirements. And different service strategies will need to be configured according to the stock and incremental data according to different modules and different scenarios. Based on the above analysis and considerations, the design practice of the acquisition and preprocessing engine is configured in 8 dimensions according to the requirements of this project.

Data Modeling. The selection of leased assets has a wide range and complex dimensions. With the development of industrial technology, it also brings uncertainty to the data dimensions and attributes of "things". Data modeling should first meet the existing management needs, and leave flexibility in order to respond to and accommodate the possibilities of the future [2].

Platform Hierarchical Model. In building platform architecture, in order to meet the requirements of different levels of data, the horizontal hierarchical model design reference DMBOK 2.0 chapter 11 data warehouse and business intelligence concept architecture diagram. Considering the difference in magnitude between the platform and the data warehouse, only a three-tier architecture is applied to the layered model to facilitate management and meet requirements.

Source Data Layer: used to store basic data of satellite, Internet of Things, and internal and external system after collection and preprocessing. At this time, the data application direction is not clear, so this layer is designed in the form of native storage. In the future, the layer can continue to expand according to the richness of docking external data sources.

Theme Fusion Layer: This layer is mainly used to further integrate and summarize data, combine with the output results of data models and data standards, and integrate data by wide table design. This layer can solve the integration problem between different data sources by completing the asset data index, and normalize the data. With the implementation of data standards in this layer, data items with different terms but consistent meanings can be modeled and consolidated. This layer can also solve the problem of the master data version of assets. The data after governance can provide a trusted and unified data version for the subsequent application market layer. In the future, the data models and standards of this layer will be controlled according to the process of planning, establishment, review and maintenance. Only when the field range cannot cover the actual situation, can they be revised through consultation between technology and business personnel.

Application Market Layer: according to the needs of the platform, it provides users with data after processing and reorganization based on the theme fusion layer and the paste source data layer, and is designed and developed with the idea of demand oriented and application oriented. The marts are independent and can be developed independently, such as risk market, market value market and ledger market, to meet users' real needs for leased asset management.

Data Subject Model Practice. Key points of modeling design: According to the principle of PRISM in DMBOK2.0, performance and usability, reusability, integrity, security and maintainability should be considered when planning the design of leased asset data model. As a description of the data entities involved in the leased asset platform, the data model should be able to describe the meaning, specifications, mapping relationships, and associations and rules with other entities. As a landing exploration of micro governance concept, data governance must follow the overall data architecture. In particular, it should be noted that the data model of a specific platform should refer to and undertake enterprise level data models, especially the granularity of entities and the association between subject domains, to avoid inconsistent and difficult understanding of the organization's understanding of data.

Explore the design of the lease asset meta model: the meta model is the data about data describing the data, mainly describing the information of the data attributes. The solution proposed to deal with the complex format of the lease asset and the inability to effectively integrate it into one model is to manage the data with an overall model framework, which can be used to describe the unknown type of data even if it appears in the future. For example, no matter how the equipment changes, there should always be data in the dimensions of ownership, operation, value and alert.

Thinking of Modeling Practice. Given that the data modeling will affect the design of the physical data model, and can further develop the data standards and collect the metadata information based on the data model, it can be said that the thinking of the data model determines the results of the project, so it should be comprehensively considered when planning the data modeling work. In the development and construction of the platform, data modeling should be focused on, and business review and technical review should be introduced when necessary.

Data Standard Practice. Although data standards have no independent chapters in DMBOK 2.0, they are discussed in the chapters of data modeling and design, metadata management and other. In this micro-governance practice, we briefly describe how to establish the data standard, mainly from the two perspectives: standard elements and standard maintenance process.

Elements to be Covered by the Data Standards. The work of data standardization should start from sorting out the data elements between the internal and external systems. The scope of the elements should include the naming, definition, type, value domain, calculation method, interpretation, authoritative system and other elements of the data items. While establishing data standards, data quality verification rules should also be determined, including the principles of integrity, timeliness, relevance and accuracy, to ensure the orderly production of subsequent data according to the standards.

Data Standard Maintenance Process. The revision of data standards requires process control with certain seriousness. The following two links should be mainly considered in the design of the process:

Standard Research: everything starts from the actual situation. When researching on data standards attention should be paid to the existing reference documents of national standards or industry standards, especially the financial industry, medical care and other relatively mature industries. Meanwhile attention should be paid to the universality and reference of data standards.

Approval and Confirmation: the opinions of suppliers and users should be fully considered in the review, and the opinions of relevant parties should be consulted before the implementation after the revision.

Practice Summary of Data Standards. Generally speaking, data standards also have two collection modes: "top to bottom" and "bottom to top". The former is unified by the top level of the organization and practiced by various systems. Its advantages are fast promotion and easy management of standards. Its disadvantages are that it is difficult to ensure high-quality collection standards in the early stage, but it is not conducive to data management if it is only promoted in a hurry. The latter is formed by collecting and summarizing the current situation of each system construction. The advantage is that the establishment of data standards is more consistent with the actual needs. The lack is that if the historical system is involved, the research is difficult, and it is easy to fall into the "Rashomon" in the data definition and cannot make a decision.

The revision of data standards will lead to a new round of data correction and system marking work, and the establishment of good data standards and reference implementation will bring competitive advantages to data management and even enterprises. From a strategic point of view, actual needs and learned from excellent experience should be combined to ensure that data standards are forward-looking, put an end to formalism.

3.5 Achievement and Value Realization of Micro-governance

By combining the data micro governance in the implementation of the platform, leasing assets online management platform initially realized the first phase of goals to improve management efficiency and to solve the pain points of rental data management. It is the excellent practice to combine the heterogeneous data from Internet of things and satellite with date from financial leasing business, which improves to a great extent the level of leasing assets management ability. It is a solid step taken for enterprises digital transformation and for the exploration of AI asset management. The implementation effect of micro-governance is reflected in the following aspects.

Strengthen the Financial Attribute of Leased Assets. Good data management ability is not only reflected in enterprise operation, but also has gradually played a prominent role in asset trading in recent years. In the financial leasing business, asset securitization (ABS) is a refinancing behavior based on lease claims, which requires investors to bear certain risks. Through effective integration of data intelligence, it can prove the real right, operating capacity, profitability of leased assets to investors, and even the business situation of enterprises, which is conducive to proving the value of leased assets and promoting asset trading. Realizing the goal of asset digitalization will help the value transformation of leased assets from physical assets, digital assets to financial assets.

Reduce Operational Risk and Improve Management Efficiency. Through the establishment of the management capability by means of the Internet of Things and integrated display, an asset management platform covering the whole life cycle of the registration, transaction, use, maintenance and destruction of leased items has been implemented. With the help of data grasp and analysis, it effectively solves the difficulties in traditional asset management, such as rights confirmation, valuation, supervision and disposal, and helps finance leasing companies achieve the management goal of more than 80% of assets digitalization. In the future, as a link of industry finance integration and industry asset integration, asset data and will cooperate with all departments of the company to comprehensively improve and improve the digital transformation goal.

Supporting Management and Operation Decisions. With the deepening application and development of the leased asset data domain, and in combination with other high-quality internal and external data after micro governance, such as data in different fields such as business, financial report, bank research, and market, it is possible to deeply manage and analyze market and enterprise intelligence, quantify macro industry and enterprise risk management indicators, and assist in full link intelligent management and decision-making before, during, and after leasing [3].

3.6 Summary

Data management, as the basis of digital transformation, has been mentioned many times in recent years. If data is not effectively managed, any platform and system can only be called "digital on paper", which will not help enterprises improve efficiency, but will have to do two jobs online and offline at the same time because of responding to the call of digitalization. The resource consumption is greater than before, let alone digital empowerment.

Enterprises must pay attention to data governance, and to the effective landing of data governance practice as well, to "lay a position" for the exploration of organization's data governance strategy, and to quickly build confidence. Data governance is not only a matter of the information technology department, but involves the business, system, process and many other aspects. The successful data governance must be of multiple measures at the same time, and of all staff participation. Only through unremitting efforts and continuous promotion can we do a good job in data governance.

4 Outlook and Thinking

In this practice, under the guidance of data governance system, digital twins and other systems and concepts, the goal of digitalizing leased assets has been achieved by using three-dimensional technical means such as network collection, Internet of Things, satellite data, etc. In the future, after meeting compliance requirements and property management needs, we should continue to deepen the value-added scenarios of assets and different fields, and rely on high-quality data and digital technology to give play to the value of data, Expand the application scope of data services, and provide more digital cases for promoting the digital reform of the financial leasing industry.

4.1 Remote Intelligent Due Diligence

In the review and summary of this project, it is found that FinTech has an obvious enabling role in the due diligence work. In the future, it is hoped to further explore the intelligent remote due diligence based on the existing applications, combined with RPA, face recognition, blockchain and other technologies. Improve the convenience by means of science and technology, reduce the investigation error caused by manual judgment, improve the production efficiency and strengthen the front and rear linkage in the due diligence process.

4.2 ESG Rating Study

At present, the platform has initially introduced, analyzed and applied aerospace satellite data. In recent years, many financial companies have begun to actively explore research based on environmental protection and carbon neutralization. The future research direction will consider whether the climate data overlay analysis model can be obtained by satellite, build the risk assessment capability based on ESG indicators, combine ESG related indicators with the review process, and optimize the project selection logic. After further introducing ESG public opinion monitoring, corporate social responsibility will be gradually implemented while responding to environmental protection strategies.

4.3 Digital Scene Mining

With the development of the financial leasing industry, both the management mode and the development logic have changed greatly. However, the essence and core logic of leasing remain unchanged. If we can find a suitable scenario entry point and introduce more financial technology on the basis of reliable data, the future benefits will be incalculable.

At present, due to the regulatory impact, the financial leverage of commercial finance leasing companies is greatly limited. Through quantitative analysis, funds can be deployed to the highest income business areas; Assist the management to focus on strategic layout through accurate analysis of the industry; If the Internet of Things and big data can be integrated into the transaction scheme or leasing model selection and other scenarios, it can effectively promote the circulation of assets, value preservation and appreciation.

What is lacking in the future is not new technology, but how to effectively combine the application with the business scenario. While continuously accumulating experience and algorithms, we should fully combine the characteristics of supply chain finance, help realize digital supply chain finance, and effectively reflect the service and promotion of financial leasing to the real industry.

References

1. The People's Bank of China: Guidelines for financial data capacity building: JR/T0218-2021 (2021)
2. Watson, H.J., Fuller, C., Ariyachandra, T.: Data warehouse governance: best practices at Blue Cross and Blue Shield of North Carolina. Decis. Support Syst. **38**(3), 435–450 (2004)
3. Wei, L.: Do a good job in data governance to promote digital transformation. Chin. Finance **2020**(01), 43–45 (2020)

How to Build an Efficient Data Team

Rui Zhao[✉]

ShubeiYunji (Beijing) Technology Co., Ltd., Beijing, China
18624097733@qq.com

Abstract. Organization Capability (OC) is the basis for the survival of enterprises. Today, the CDO and its team are the cost center responsible for establishing and tracking compliance with policies, standards, and procedures to manage data and ensure its high quality. Going forward, the CDO and its team operate as a business unit with P & L responsibility. Working with business teams, the unit is responsible for conceptualizing new ways to use data, developing a data strategy for the overall enterprise (and embedding it as part of the business strategy), and incubating new revenue streams by monetizing data services and data sharing. This article will focus on the core elements of organizational capability (i.e., employees) to examine how the Chief Data Officer (CDO) should build an efficient data team to build data-driven organizational capabilities and maintain the continuous success of the enterprise.

Keywords: Chief Data Officer (CDO) · CDO Office (CO) · Organizational Capacity (OC)

1 Introduction

The Yang Triangle framework of organizational capability is a management tool to enhance the soft power of enterprises and the combat effectiveness of teams. The Yang Triangle framework of organizational capability consists of the central organizational capability and the peripheral employee competence, employee thinking, and employee governance [1].

Employee competence, that is, all employees of an enterprise must have the knowledge, skills and qualities to build the required organizational competence.

Employee thinking, that is, to build the thinking mode of employees, so that the things they care about, pursue and value in their daily work match the data-driven organizational capabilities needed by enterprises. Employee governance, that is, the enterprise must also provide effective management support and resources to allow these talents to play a full role in building data-driven organizational capabilities. If organizational capacity is to be solid, these three pillars must be built in accordance with two principles:

1) Matching principle: the focus of each of the three pillars must be aligned with its organizational capacity [1];
2) Balance principle: All three pillars should be equally strong, not just one or two of them [1] (Fig. 1).

K. Ye and L.-J. Zhang (Eds.): CLOUD 2022, LNCS 13731, pp. 96–108, 2022.
https://doi.org/10.1007/978-3-031-23498-9_8

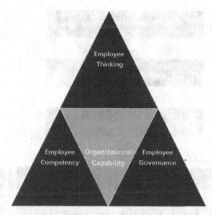

Fig. 1. The Yang Triangle framework of organizational capacity [1]

As the requirements described in Yang Triangle framework, the role of the Chief Data Officer (CDO) is on the rise, CDOs require a variety of capabilities, including technical, business, management, strategy, and more. This article discusses CDO survival tips in organizations and CDO Office (CO) capacity building. At this basis we can explore how CDOs build organizational employee capabilities and data literacy and give the CDO's short-term and long-term strategic plans in the organization.

2 CDO and Organizational Capability

Establishing a Chief Data Officer (CDO) system and building an efficient CDO Office (CO) team are to construct data-driven organizational capabilities [12] and sustain the success of the organization. These are necessary for the organization [2, 13]. CDOs should focus on recruiting and developing bridge talents for COs who understand both business and technology. Competency requirements can refer to the job description in is CDO Job Description [1, 2].

CDOs need to focus on the following points when building CO's employee capacity:

1) Type of talent. As far as I can see, bridge-type people are more likely to have an IT background than a business background.
2) Talent mentality. CO should exist as a bridge between business and technology, and try to find the best breakthrough, such as the vague area between technology and business. Establish a relationship of trust, accumulate small wins into big wins, and gradually exaggerate influence through the spread of power.
3) Talent positioning. The top executive leader (CEO) of the enterprise should support CDO and CO as much as possible, and one of the important manifestations is to give full title.

2.1 Team Capability

The capability planning model can help enterprises systematically plan talents, as shown in Fig. 2. It mainly considers three issues: capability determination, capability review, and capability building.

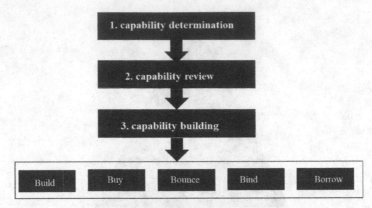

Fig. 2. Capacity planning model [1]

2.1.1 Capability Determination

Enterprise's talent capability is equal to professional capability and core capability [15, 16]. The process of building a capability model generally includes five steps, as shown in the following Fig. 3: 1) Focus on interview and collection; 2) Focus on integration and ranking; 3) Focus on discussion and confirmation; 4) Focus on clarity and concreteness; 5) Focusing on publication and application.

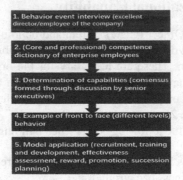

Fig. 3. Flow chart of building the capability model [1]

• Professional competency.

The professional competency model can be constructed through the process described in Fig. 3. An example is given here.

1) CO's key team capabilities mainly include eight aspects: consulting services; data strategy; data investment; data standards; data management; diplomatic communication; data literacy; and data development.

2) The CO function consists of six main roles: data governance; data language; data science; data security; data management; and data services.

3) Common CO employee skills, including 4 areas: best practices; information technology; data science; management capabilities.

4) CO employees put forward the most basic qualification requirements, which mainly include two aspects [7]:

(1) Education:

    A. Major: Computer Science/Information Engineering, Business Administration/MBA (optional);
    B. Education: Junior College/Bachelor/Master/Doctor;
    C. Certification: CCDO/CDGP/CDGA/CDMP/CBIP/CPMP.

(2) Experience:

    A. Cross-sectorial work experience;
    B. Project management experience (waterfall, agile);
    C. Experience in data governance and big data projects;
    D. Experience in data security and data privacy projects;
    E. Solutions, consulting and training experience.

- Core competency
- Core competency models can also be constructed through the process described in Fig. 3. In addition to the general core competencies such as IQ (intelligence quotient) and EQ (emotional quotient), there should also be the unique core competence needs of enterprises.

2.1.2 Capability Review

This step requires a current situation analysis, a goal analysis, and a gap analysis. Refer to the following Table 1 for examples:

2.1.3 Capability Building

It mainly solves the problem of how to improve the capability of talents. Training, recruitment, elimination, retention and borrowing are recommended.

2.2 Team Thinking

Team thinking focuses on how to reshape the consistent thinking mode of employees [1, 17].

2.2.1 Cultural Values

The reshaping of team thinking is divided into three steps (Fig. 4):

Table 1. Capability gap analysis.

Competency type	Existing capacity	Capacity gap	Future needs
Professional competency	Data governance experts: 2 Data quality experts: 3 Data warehouse experts: 3 Business intelligence expert: 1 DBA: 2	In terms of quantity: Data governance experts: -3 Data quality expert: -1 Master Data Specialist:-1 Metadata expert: -1 Data warehouse expert: -1 Business intelligence experts: -4 DBA:-2	Data governance experts: 5 Data quality experts: 4 Master data expert: 1 person Metadata expert: 1 person Data warehouse experts: 4 Business intelligence experts: 4 DBA: 4
Core competency	1. Integrity: 4.0 2. Learning ability: 3.3 3. Conscientiousness: 5.0 4. Customer orientation: 5.0 5. In pursuit of excellence: 4.2 6. Teamwork: 5.0 7. Innovation and change: 4.6	Qualitative aspects: Integrity and honesty Ability to learn The pursuit of excellence Innovation and change	1. Integrity: 5.0 2. Learning ability: 4.0 3. Conscientiousness: 5.0 4. Customer orientation: 5.0 5. In pursuit of excellence: 4.5 6. Teamwork: 5.0 7. Innovation and Change: 5.0

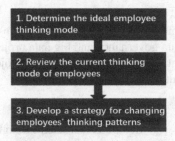

Fig. 4. Ways to reshape employees' mindset [1]

Determining the target mindset, the current mindset needs of employees are to build data-driven organizational capabilities; reviewing the current mindset, that is to conduct a current assessment of the mindset of current CO and employees throughout the enterprise and conduct a gap analysis, develop a change strategy and implement it.

2.2.2 Establishing Values

The enterprise needs to establish the cultural values and code of conduct of employees. The establishment process is similar to the competency building model in Sect. 2.1, but there is a difference in Step 5. Its application is mainly in publicity, training, practice, performance appraisal, reward, promotion and other aspects.

2.2.3 Reshaping Values

In order to successfully reshape the team thinking mode, enterprises mainly include:

1) Executives' words and deeds: "What the boss does is better than what the boss says" [1, 2];

2) Data literacy: improve the data literacy of the whole employee of the enterprise and completely eliminate data illiteracy [5];
3) Supporting tools: elimination mechanism, equity incentive, promotion and salary increase, etc.

2.3 Team Governance

Team governance should solve the problem of employee tolerance, that is what kind of structure, resources and processes the enterprise needs [1, 14].

2.3.1 Data Team Architecture

CO is more suitable to adopt a market-oriented ecological organizational structure and become a network model composed of a large platform and many small business teams. Let the invisible beacon of market demand guide the direction of action of enterprises and teams; ecology is to show enough vitality [1, 6].

An example is shown in the following Fig. 5:

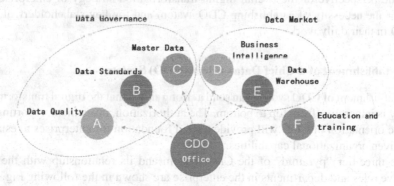

Fig. 5. Example of market-oriented ecological organization structure of CDO office

In the figure, A–F are all project teams, and ABC and DE are also two independent project sets, and all or part of the teams belong to CO.

2.3.2 Team Position Setting

For CO, I would like to add two more major generic roles:

1) Project Manager:

    (1) Major: Computer Science/Information Engineering, Business Administration/MBA [7];
    (2) Education: Junior College/Bachelor/Master/Doctor;
    (3) Certification: CPMP (required)/CCDO/CDGP/CDMP/CDGA/CBIP;
    (4) Experience: 10 + years, including 5 + years in project management and 5 + years in data.

2) HR Specialist:

(1) Major: Computer Science/Information Engineering, HR;
(2) Education: Junior College/Bachelor/Master/Doctor;
(3) Certification: CDGP/CDMP/CDGA;
(4) Experience: 5 + years, including 3 + years of data experience.

Note: In the initial stage of CO establishment, it is recommended that PM be held by a senior business specialist or data governance expert, while HR can be held by an HR specialist in the human resources department, but they must also be experts in data or have received necessary training [1]. When the CO team is large, it is recommended to set up a dedicated PM and HR, and they must have expert capabilities and best practices in data management.

3 How to Implement Organizational Capability

From the perspective of the overall digital transformation strategy of enterprises, we consider the necessity of establishing CDO system and the key stakeholders of CDO and CO in their daily work.

3.1 Establishment of a Chief Data Officer (CDO) System

The establishment of CDO system can send a strong signal that the digital transformation strategy is imperative from top to bottom. The authorization, investment, reporting path and role orientation of CDO will provide a solid foundation for enterprises to establish data-driven organizational capabilities.

The three-tier "pyramid" of the CDO system and its relationship with the main executive roles and departments in the enterprise are shown in the following Fig. 6.

3.2 Synergy of Four Key Groups

The establishment of data-driven organizational capacity depends on four key groups of stakeholders: CEO, CDO, HR Specialist, Supervisors at all levels.

1) CEOs and executives need to initiate and advocate the CDO system and maintain confidence and unity of words and deeds.
2) The CO is expected to contribute professional competence to the cultural values and code of conduct of the enterprise.
3) As an integral part of CO, HR specialists are the foundation and core strength for building employee capabilities, reshaping employee thinking and establishing employee governance.
4) Supervisors at all levels have the greatest and most direct influence and force on grass-roots employees, and they themselves must grow rapidly.

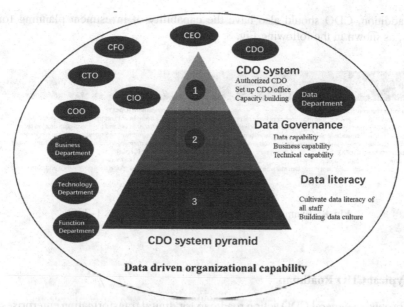

Fig. 6. Relationship between CDO institutional pyramid and data-driven organizational capability [5]

4   CDO Roadmap

The initial phase of the CDO (100 or 90 days) will be the key to its success. The CDO provides a methodology based on best practices [8, 9, 11].

4.1   IsCDO Roadmap Theory

In the CDO 90-day Action Plan of is CDO, the first 90 days of CDO are divided into three stages: 30/60/90. See the Fig. 7 below:

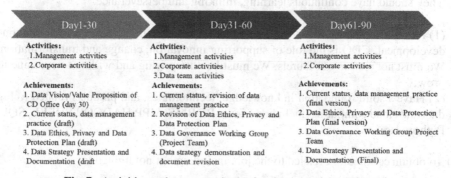

Fig. 7. Activities and outcomes in the first 90 days of the CDO [8]

In addition, CDO should also have the capability of investment planning for 1–2 years, as shown in the following Fig. 8:

Fig. 8. Example of investment plan for CDO years 1–2 [8]

4.2 Typical CDO Roadmap

Here I propose a general CDO action roadmap for digital transformation enterprises. We start with how to be a CDO and how to build trust by achieving short-term wins, and finally we need sustained focus to achieve long-term wins [6].

4.2.1 How to Become a CDO

1) I have always argued that people in computer science or information engineering are better suited to CDO (and CO) roles. The main reason is that people with IT (information technology) basic knowledge system generally have good abstract thinking capability and strong learning capability. For non-computer science and information engineering professionals, I suggest completing the IT knowledge system, including computer principle, microcomputer principle, operating system principle, database principle, network basic theory, SQL/Python programming language, etc., which can also become an excellent CDO.

2) They should have continuous learning, thinking and perseverance.

(1) New technologies, new ideas and new tools are still in the process of continuous development. CDO is the role of supporting innovation, change and transformation. We must not rest on our laurels. We must be enterprising and willing to continue to grow;

(2) Have a solid foundation in knowledge, technologies, and products related to big data and cloud computing, including Linux, RDBMS, MPP, HADOOP, SHELL, SQL, Python, etc.

3) To obtain certification related to the job, including but not limited to:

(1) Relevant certification of DAMA China (International) DAMA-DMBOK knowledge system: CDGA/CDGP/CDMP/CCDO, etc.;

(2) Foreign CDO related certification: CCDO of MIT iCDO & IQ/CDataO of Carnegie Mellon, etc.;

(3) Project management certification: PMI's PMP and PMI-ACP, etc.;

(4) Ministry of Industry and Information Technology's soft test related certification: information system management engineer, system integration project management engineer, and information security engineer.

4.2.2 Win a Short-Term Victory

1) There are two main things to do before taking office [9]:

(1) Understand the organization's business, technology, cultural values, code of conduct, etc.;

(2) Establish informal communication with key stakeholders and demonstrate competencies and accomplishments.

2) **Day 1**, go through formalities and get acquainted with key stakeholders:

(1) Understand the company's procedures and receive the necessary training;

(2) Meet with the direct supervisor to establish communication channels and reporting mechanism;

(3) Meet with immediate subordinates to establish lines of communication and demonstrate competencies and accomplishments.

3) **Week 1**, establish communication and mutual understanding with key stakeholders:

(1) Meet with HR specialists to get to know each other and establish communication channels;

(2) Meet with other key stakeholders to get to know each other and establish lines of communication.

4) **In the first month**, collect requirements and maintain communication with the direct supervisor and HR:

(1) Collect and record the real needs of key/major stakeholders;

(2) Consolidate requirements, analyze them, and prioritize them initially;

(3) Develop solutions and personnel capacity and quantity requirements;

(4) Personnel status assessment and gap analysis, develop personnel demand plan;

(5) Cooperate with HR to start personnel recruitment and training.

5) **Q1**, build CO and build trust:

(1) Recruit necessary personnel and train new and existing personnel;

(2) According to the business strategy, establish the data strategy and align the digital transformation strategy;

(3) Establish and promote CO's cultural values and code of conduct;

(4) Deliver small projects with low risk and quick results to build trust;
(5) Accumulate small wins for big wins and establish the status of CDO and CO.

4.2.3   Win a Long-Term Victory

1) In the first half year, establish CO data-driven organizational capabilities.

(1) CO establishes a unified cultural values and code of conduct;
(2) CO has complete organizational system, good coordination of personnel and combat effectiveness;
(3) Large-scale projects can be launched to promote the implementation of the digital transformation strategy.

2) In the first year, build basic data and digital capabilities, and improve organizational data literacy.

(1) Establish data governance platform, build data governance capabilities, and ensure data quality;
(2) Establish master data and reference data platforms, promote data standards and data sharing;
(3) Build data warehouse/data lake and establish data analysis capability.

3) In the second year, we will promote the automation/intellectualization of data assets and digital transformation.

(1) Open up global data, unify data standards and ensure high quality of data;
(2) Establish a data science team to promote data asset realization and decision-making capabilities;
(3) Support digital transformation and reshape business model with data-driven organizational capabilities.

4) After the third year, continue to build data-driven organizational capacity and create value.

(1) CO team should keep innovative spirit, agile thinking and enterprising spirit;
(2) In-depth use of AI, ML and other emerging technologies;
(3) Form a team and business model with self-renewal and self-improvement capabilities.

5   Conclusion

Today, the CDO and its team are the cost center responsible for establishing and tracking compliance with policies, standards, and procedures to manage data and ensure its high quality. Going forward, the CDO and its team operate as a business unit with P & L responsibility. Working with business teams, the unit is responsible for conceptualizing new ways to use data, developing a data strategy for the overall enterprise (and embedding it as part of the business strategy), and incubating new revenue streams by monetizing data services and data sharing.

Daily applications. Healthcare Industry CDOs work with business units to deliver new subscription-based services to patients, payers, and providers that improve patient outcomes. These services may include customized treatment plans, more accurate labeling of incorrectly coded medical transactions, and improved drug safety [10]. Bank Finance Industry CDOs commercialize internal data-oriented services such as fraud monitoring and anti-money laundering services on behalf of government agencies and other partners [10]. Consumer Products Industry CDOs work with sales teams to use data to drive sales conversion and share responsibility for meeting target metrics [10].

Key enablers. It Popularizes data knowledge among business unit leaders and their teams to create the energy and urgency to engage with CDOs and their teams. An economic model, such as an automated P & L tracker, used to identify and attribute data and costs. It needs top data talent with innovative vision. It adopts the incubator operation mode of venture capital to support experiments and innovations.

How do we start For CDOs, they should start having conversations with business unit leaders to identify opportunities to use data to drive business value. And they develop overall priorities based on scorecards and metrics, covering organizational health, talent and culture, and data quality [10]. They enhance ethical use of data to ensure that new revenue-generating data services are aligned with company values and culture.

References

1. Guoan, Y.: Gene of Change and Digital Intelligence Innovation - How Chinese Enterprises Embrace Digital Transformation. CITIC Press, Beijng (2021)
2. Henderson, D., Earley, S., Sebastian-Coleman, L.: Data Management Body of Knowledge, 2nd edn. Technics Publications, USA (2017)
3. Wang, R.Y.: CDO Workbook, vol. 1. MIT Chief Data Officer & Information Quality Program, USA (2019)
4. Treder, M.: CDO Management Handbook. Apress, Germany (2020)
5. Aiken, P., Harbor, T.: Data Literacy. Technics Publications, USA (2021)
6. Aiken, P.: CDO Journey. Technics Publications, USA (2021)
7. Abate, R., Villar, M.: CDO Job Description. R2.0. isCDO, USA (2021)
8. Abate, R.: CDO 90-Day Action Plan. R1.6. isCDO, USA (2021)
9. Logan, D., White, A., Bugajski, J.: CDO First 100 Days Roadmap 2017. Gartner, USA (2017)
10. Assur, N., Rowshankish, K.: The Data-Driven Enterprise 2025. McKinsey, USA (2022)
11. Aiken, P., Gorman, M.: Creating the Right Conditions for CDO Success - ScienceDirect. The Case for the Chief Data Officer 51–65 (2013)
12. Dud, L.: The Organizational Capability: Competing from the Inside Out. Wiley, New York (1990)
13. Lee, J.J., Yoon, H.: A comparative study of technological learning and organizational capability development in complex products systems: distinctive paths of three latecomers in military aircraft industry. Res. Policy 44(7), 1296–1313 (2015)
14. Zhang, L.F., Zeng, D.M., Zhang, Y.S.: Empirical Research on R&D Team's Governance in High-Tech Enterprises. Scientific Management Research (2004)

15. Moreira, M.E.: Evaluating agile, engineering, and team capability. In: Being Agile, pp. 131–138. Apress, Berkeley (2013). https://doi.org/10.1007/978-1-4302-5840-7_13
16. Xu, X., Zhang, W., Barkhi, R.: IT infrastructure capabilities and IT project success: a development team perspective. Inf. Technol. Manage. **11**, 123–142 (2010). https://doi.org/10.1007/s10799-010-0072-3
17. Nonose, K., Kanno, T., Furuta, K.: A team cognition model derived from an analysis of reflection on cooperation. Cogn. Tech. Work **14**, 83–92 (2012). https://doi.org/10.1007/s10111-011-0179-2

A Novel Unsupervised Anomaly Detection Approach Using Neural Transformation in Cloud Environment

Rui Zhang[1], Juan Chen[1], Yujia Song[1], Wenyu Shan[1], Peng Chen[1(✉)], and Yunni Xia[2(✉)]

[1] School of Computer and Software Engineering, Xihua University, Chengdu, China
chenpeng@mail.xhu.edu.cn
[2] College of Computer Science, Chongqing University, Chongqing, China
xiayunni@hotmail.com

Abstract. As a new way of computing on the Internet, cloud computing has completely changed the abstraction and utilization of computing
infrastructure and is favored by users of significant enterprises. Therefore,
various large-scale cloud computing systems have emerged. Cloud computing systems capture real-time indicators in the form of multivariate
time series. Therefore, it is necessary and valuable to do multivariate time
series anomaly detection in the cloud computing system. However, because
the data monitored in the cloud computing system is massive, redundant,
contains noise and missing values, and is accompanied by the random-
ness and scarcity of anomalies, anomaly detection in the cloud computing system will generate high computational costs and the challenge of
uncertain detection results. To solve these problems, we use neural transformation (NT) for anomaly detection, that is, Neural Transformation-
Encoding-Auto Regression (NT-E-AR). NT-E-AR uses NT to generate
different transformation views from the input data. Convolutional Long-
Short Term Memory (ConvLSTM) encoding network and Autoregressive Long-Short Term Memory (LSTM) are combined to extract Spatio-
Temporal features of time series data to achieve better anomaly detection
capability. Extensive experiments show that NT-E-AR consistently outperforms all baselines on three open datasets and achieves an average F1
(0.772), increasing the average accuracy by 16.52%.

Keywords: Cloud computing system · Multivariate time series ·
Neural transformation · Anomaly detection

1 Introduction

As more and more social resources are networked and digitized, big data comes
into being. The storage and calculation of massive data force the innovation of
technology. As one of the most rapid technologies to adapt to the era of big data,

R. Zhang and J. Chen—These authors contributed to the work equllly and should be
regarded as co-first authors.

cloud computing has become more and more popular. Cloud computing relies on the cloud computing system, and the performance of the cloud computing system dramatically affects our daily life. Due to the richness of time series data in cloud computing systems and the importance of time series performance metrics in monitoring cloud services, the demand for time series anomaly detection methods has become huge [1].

Time series anomaly detection has always been a hot research field for researchers [2]. It is widely used in cloud computing systems. For example, anomaly detection of time series in a cloud computing system is to detect anomalies generated by massive and high-dimensional time series data to ensure the regular operation of the platform [3].

Multivariate time series data collected in real-time in cloud computing systems are usually massive and high-dimensional. And the anomalies are infrequent and random. The existing methods are not very effective in dealing with such problems. For example, Local Neural Transformation (LNT) [4] combines with Contrastive Predictive Coding (CPC) [5] to extract time series temporal features to detect anomalies. However, LNT does not consider the spatial features of multivariate time series but only obtains temporal features, resulting in incomplete extraction of features. Inspired by LNT, we combine NT, ConvLSTM, and autoregressive LSTM [6] to account for the spatial features of multivariate time series. As a result, the extracted features can fully represent the original data and improve the ability of anomaly detection.

In the NT-E-AR model, we first use NT to obtain transformation views representing different aspects of data. Then, the transformation views pass through ConvLSTM [7] to extract the Spatio-Temporal features of time series data. Finally, at the end of the model, to further extract helpful information and make predictions, autoregressive LSTM is used to improve the anomaly detection ability of the model.

To summarize, the main contributions of our work are:

(1) We propose an unsupervised anomaly detection model (NT-E-AR) based on NT, which can effectively detect anomalies in cloud computing systems. NT-E-AR can achieve good performance in three open datasets.
(2) We use NT to realize the anomaly detection ability of complex time series in a cloud computing system and improve the robustness of the model.
(3) We use ConvLSTM and autoregressive LSTM networks to extract temporal and spatial features from the transformation view, integrating historical information to guide predictions.

2   Related Work

Unsupervised anomaly detection based on deep learning on multivariate time series data is challenging, and various methods have been developed over the past few years.

LSTM NDT [8] proposes an unsupervised method based on a non-parametric dynamic threshold and cooperates with LSTM to detect the anomaly of telemetry data returned from spacecraft, reducing operation engineers' monitoring burden and operational risks. MSCRED [9] model reconstructs the signature matrix using a convolutional encoder and decoder, and uses the residual signature matrix to detect anomalies. DAGMM [10] is an end-to-end model and uses a deep auto-encoder Gaussian mixture model to retain critical information of the input sample in low-dimensional space (dimensionality reduction operation). USAD [11] is proposed to use an autoencoder to detect anomalies in multivariate time series and cooperates with adversarial training to isolate anomalies and speeds up model training. TranAD [12] is a deep transformer network-based anomaly detection model that uses an attention-based sequence encoder to enable fast inference of knowledge about temporal trends. GDN [13] utilizes a GNN to learn correlations in data and outputs anomaly scores using attention-based prediction and deviation scoring.VAE-GAN [14] uses LSTM as the model's encoder, generator, and discriminator to train the three together. Finally, the time series anomaly is detected according to the reconstruction error and the discriminant result.

3   OUR METHOD: NT-E-AR

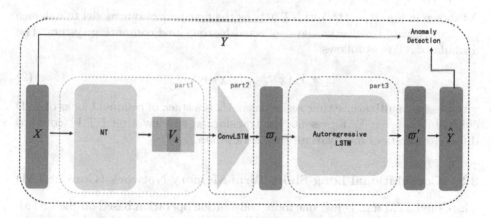

Fig. 1. NT-E-AR architecture. (part1) represents the Neural Transformation; (part2) represents the ConvLSTM; (part3) represents the Autoregressive LSTM network. (The error between Y and $\hat{Y}$ represents the anomaly detection of the whole model.)

We input multivariate time series data $X = (x_1, ..., x_n)^T \in R^{n \times T}$ into the model, where T is the dimension of the input data and n is the number of input data. When the input data passes through the model, a label vector $Y = (y_1, ..., y_n) \in R^{n \times 1}$ is generated, where $y_i \in \{0, 1\}$ represents whether the i-th time point is abnormal, 0 represents no abnormality, and 1 represents abnormal.

We use mean-variance normalization to process the data input into the model so that all features have the same metric. X_{scale} is expressed as follows:

$$X_{scale} = \frac{X - X_\mu}{X_S} \tag{1}$$

where X_μ represents the average, and X_S represents the standard deviation.

3.1 NT-E-AR Architecture

Our model is shown in Fig. 1. To obtain different transformation views V, the time series data are first input into the NT. ConvLSTM encoder then separates different views and extracts features from V. Finally, the potential representation ϖ obtained by the encoder is input into the autoregressive LSTM to get the predicted value. Our abnormal score is the difference between the actual and predicted values, and the abnormal score above the threshold is our abnormal point.

3.2 Neural Transformation(NT)

As shown in Fig. 1(part1), our NT acts as the first part of our model to enhance the multivariate time series data collected by the cloud computing system. The formula of NT is as follows:

$$V_k(\chi) := M_k(\chi) + \chi \tag{2}$$

χ represents multivariate time series data; M_k is a stack of residual blocks of a 2D consvolution layer; V_k represents the transformation view after NT, V_k contains different aspects of multivariate time series data.

3.3 Convolutional Long-Short Term Memory Network (ConvLSTM)

The ConvLSTM unit is just one more convolution operation based on the LSTM. As shown in Fig. 1(part2), so that both spatial and temporal features can be extracted.

Through the ConvLSTM layer, the potential representation is expressed as:

$$\varpi_i = g_{enc}(V_k) \tag{3}$$

where V_k represents all transformation views and ϖ_i represents the extracted potential representation.

In this work, we use an exponential linear unit (ELU) [15] as the activation function and two ConvLSTM layers, each set to 64 kernels of size 1×3.

3.4   Autoregressive Long Short Term Memory Network (LSTM)

The autoregressive LSTM network part, shown in Fig. 1(part3), is in the model's last part and integrates the features of all the potential representations $\varpi'_{\leqslant i}$ obtained earlier and makes predictions for the next step. Y_{i+1} is expressed as :

$$Y_{i+1} = g_{arm}(\varpi'_{\leqslant i}) \tag{4}$$

where $\omega'_{\leqslant i}$ represents the context information containing i and all previous, the next step after the autoregressive LSTM network prediction can fully summarize all the information above, making the forecast more accurate.

The internal structure of LSTM is as follows:

$$z_i = \sigma(\overline{W}_{XZ}X_i + \overline{W}_{HZ}H_{i-1} + \overline{W}_{CZ}°C_{i-1} + \overline{b}_Z) \tag{5}$$

$$f_i = \sigma(\overline{W}_{Xf}X_i + \overline{W}_{Hf}H_{i-1} + \overline{W}_{Cf}°C_{i-1} + \overline{b}_f) \tag{6}$$

$$C_i = z_i°\tanh(\overline{W}_{XC}X_i + \overline{W}_{HC}H_{i-1} + \overline{b}_C) + f_i°C_{i-1} \tag{7}$$

$$o_i = \sigma(\overline{W}_{XO}X_i + \overline{W}_{HO}H_{i-1} + \overline{W}_{CO}°C_i + \overline{b}_O) \tag{8}$$

$$H_i = o_i°\tanh(C_i) \tag{9}$$

where $°$ represents Hadamard product operation, σ represents the sigmoid function, all $\overline{W}$ represents weight parameters, and all $\overline{b}$ represents bias parameters.

In the LSTM unit, the activation function selects the exponential linear unit (ELU), and the number of units in the hidden layer is set to 200.

3.5   Loss Function

We define the mean square error $loss_{mse}$ between the actual value and the predicted value as our loss function, expressed as:

$$loss_{mse} = \frac{1}{n}\sum_{i=1}^{n}(y_i - \hat{y_i})^2 \tag{10}$$

where y_i is the actual value, $\hat{y_i}$ is the predicted value, and n is the number of samples.

4   Evaluation

4.1   Datasets

We use three subsets of datasets collected in real-time from cloud computing systems to verify the performance of our model. They are Secure Water Treatment SWaT [16], Mars Science Laboratory rover MSL [17], Soil Moisture Active and Passive SMAP [18]. Their details are shown in Table 1:

Table 1. Related parameters of three datasets.

Statistics	SWaT	MSL	SMAP
Data dimension	51	55	25
Train set size	5000	28317	2648
Test set size	5000	20000	7914
Abnormality rates(%)	29.2	20.5	1.3
Time granularity(s)	1	60	60

4.2   Baseline

We use four baseline methods to verify our model. They are Principal Component Analysis (PCA) [19], Variational Autoencoder (VAE) [20], Deep Transformer Networks for Anomaly Detection (TranAD) [12] and Graph Deviation Network (GDN) [13].

4.3   Implementation Details

We test the results of all models using F1, Precision, and Recall. During the model training process, we use the stochastic gradient descent method and the Adam optimizer. This experiment uses 70 epochs, 0.001 learning rate, 32 batches, and 0.2 dropout. Set a fixed number of transformations $k = 3$ in the NT part.

All of our results in the three datasets take an average of 10 results. Our experiments were conducted on a server with an NVIDIA 2080Ti graphics card, an Intel Core i9-10900K CPU at 3.70 GHz, and 32 GB of RAM. Server version of Python 3.6, GPU version of Tensorflow 1.5.0, and Python toolset pyod 0.7.4 [21].

4.4   Comparison Results

As shown in Table 2. NT-E-AR provides the best F1 in all three datasets. In SWaT, it is 24.35% better than the optimal baseline; in MSL, it is 20.95% better than the optimal baseline; and in SMAP, it is 4.27% better than the optimal baseline. Accuracy ranks second in SWaT, and the other two datasets are optimal. The recall rate performs best in SMAP, even ranking third and second in SWaT and MSL, respectively, but the difference was small. The excellent robustness shown by NT-E-AR exceeds all baseline methods. PCA is a linear dimensionality reduction algorithm. However, in the case of complete ignorance of the data, PCA transform cannot obtain better retention of data information. Therefore, the advantages of PCA cannot be reflected in complex cloud computing systems, resulting in the worst performance of PCA in the baseline.

The generative model VAE learns as many different features in the data as possible so that the generated data can represent the original data well. However, because the Decoder is too powerful, it may lead to the posterior collapse

Table 2. Anomaly detection results on three time series datasets. Gain represents the percentage of NT-E-AR that is better than the optimal baseline.

Method	SWaT			MSL			SMAP		
	F1	Pre	Rec	F1	Pre	Rec	F1	Pre	Rec
PCA	0.4527	0.2925	0.9999	0.3401	0.2049	0.9999	0.0274	0.0138	0.9999
VAE	0.4527	0.2926	0.9999	0.7166	0.5844	0.926	0.1702	0.0934	0.9999
TranAD	0.4648	0.9999	0.3028	0.0837	0.8999	0.0439	0.5459	0.3754	0.9999
GDN	0.5572	0.3881	0.9907	0.3442	0.2002	0.9306	0.033	0.0066	0.3272
NT-E-AR	0.8007	0.6816	0.978	0.9261	0.9247	0.9447	0.5886	0.4177	0.9999
Gain(%)	24.35			20.95			4.27		

problem. It fully learns the features of each input data so that the hidden distribution encoded by Encoder can be restored by Decoder when it is far away from the standard Gaussian so that the existence of hidden space is invalid.

Taken together, TranAD provides the best performance across all baseline methods (but below our model) but the worst performance in MSL. TranAD stands out from all baselines because it uses an adaptive and adversarial training process to amplify reconstruction errors, thereby reducing the omission of outliers. GDN performs moderately in all baselines but performs worst in SMAP. Because GDN uses graph structure to detect anomalies, but the lack of time series data on the temporal feature information extraction process, resulting in the effect, is not ideal compared with all baselines.

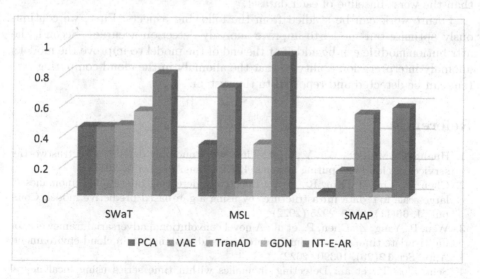

Fig. 2. All models perform F1 in three datasets. NT-E-AR is always optimal in three datasets.

Overall, as shown in Fig. 2, NT-E-AR performs best in all three datasets and shows good robustness. The performance advantage in the first two datasets is more significant than that in the third dataset. NT-E-AR can achieve better performance than the baseline because NT-E-AR can combine the temporal and spatial features of multivariate time series so that the extracted information can well represent the time series, improve the prediction ability, and thus improve the accuracy of anomaly detection.

5   Conclusion

In this paper, complex cloud computing systems will collect massive, high-dimensional time series data all the time, which will be more or less abnormal at some time. Therefore, we propose a new unsupervised model based on deep learning to detect anomalies in multivariate time series. We first use NT to obtain different transformation views of the original multivariate time series data, which contain helpful information in various aspects, and then let the integrated view enter the ConvLSTM encoder to separate different views to learn the temporal and spatial features of multivariate time series. Finally, to ensure that the values predicted by our model better reflect the original data, we use an autoregressive LSTM network to learn the long-term dependence of time series and incorporate historical information accurately.

Extensive experiments and analyses verify the effectiveness and excellent robustness of NT-E-AR. The three datasets can always show the best F1, precision, and recall performance is also relatively good, even in a dataset that is not optimal, but not much different from the optimal baseline, and always better than the worst baseline of each dataset.

Future work can be studied from the following aspects. First, we continuously optimize our model to improve anomaly detection accuracy. Second, the attribution module can be added at the end of the model to improve the model's anomaly interpretation ability so that the anomaly in the cloud computing system can be detected and reported to the system.

References

1. Huang, C., Min, G., Wu, Y., et al.: Time series anomaly detection for trustworthy services in cloud computing systems. IEEE Trans. Big Data (2017)
2. Chen, P., Liu, H., Xin, R., et al.: Effectively detecting operational anomalies in large-scale IoT data infrastructures by using a gan-based predictive model. Comput. J. **65**(11), 2909–2925 (2022)
3. Wen, P., Yang, Z., Chen, P., et al.: A novel convolutional adversarial framework for multivariate time series anomaly detection and explanation in cloud environment. Appl. Sci. **12**(20), 10390 (2022)
4. Schneider, T., et al.: Detecting anomalies within time series using local neural transformations. arXiv:2202.03944 (2022)
5. Oord, A.V.D., Li, Y., Vinyals, O.: Representation learning with contrastive predictive coding. arXiv:1807.03748 (2018)

6. Hochreiter, S., Schmidhuber, J.: Long short-term memory. Neural Comput. **9**(8), 1735–1780 (1997)
7. Shi, X., Chen, Z., Wang, H., Yeung, D.Y., Wong, W.K., Woo, W.C.: Convolutional LSTM network: a machine learning approach for precipitation nowcasting. In: Advances in Neural Information Processing Systems, vol. 28 (2015)
8. Hundman, K., Constantinou, V., Laporte, C., Colwell, I., Soderstrom, T.: Detecting spacecraft anomalies using lstms and nonparametric dynamic thresholding. In: Proceedings of the 24th ACM SIGKDD International Conference on Knowledge Discovery & Data Mining, pp. 387–395 (2018)
9. Zhang, C., et al.: A deep neural network for unsupervised anomaly detection and diagnosis in multivariate time series data. In: Proceedings of the AAAI Conference on Artificial Intelligence vol. 33, pp. 1409–1416 (2019)
10. Zong, B., Song, Q., Min, M.R., Cheng, W., Lumezanu, C., Cho, D., Chen, H.: Deep autoencoding gaussian mixture model for unsupervised anomaly detection. In: International Conference on Learning Representations (2018)
11. Audibert, J., Michiardi, P., Guyard, F., Marti, S., Zuluaga, M.A.: Usad: unsupervised anomaly detection on multivariate time series. In: Proceedings of the 26th ACM SIGKDD International Conference on Knowledge Discovery & Data Mining, pp. 3395–3404 (2020)
12. Tuli, S., Casale, G., Jennings, N.R.: Tranad: deep transformer networks for anomaly detection in multivariate time series data. arXiv:2201.07284 (2022)
13. Deng, A., Hooi, B.: Graph neural network-based anomaly detection in multivariate time series. In: Proceedings of the AAAI Conference on Artificial Intelligence, vol 35, pp. 4027–4035 (2021)
14. Niu, Z., Yu, K., Wu, X.: LSTM-based VAE-GAN for time series anomaly detection. Sensors **20**(13), 3738 (2020)
15. Clevert, D.-A., Unterthiner, T., Hochreiter, S.: Fast and accurate deep network learning by exponential linear units (elus). arXiv:1511.07289 (2015)
16. Goh, J., Adepu, S., Junejo, K.N., Mathur, A.: A dataset to support research in the design of secure water treatment systems. In: Havarneanu, G., Setola, R., Nassopoulos, H., Wolthusen, S. (eds.) CRITIS 2016. LNCS, vol. 10242, pp. 88–99. Springer, Cham (2017). https://doi.org/10.1007/978-3-319-71368-7_8
17. Grotzinger, J.P., et al.: Mars science laboratory mission and science investigation. Space Sci. Rev. **170**(1), 5–56 (2012). https://doi.org/10.1007/s11214-012-9892-2
18. O'Neill, P., Entekhabi, D., Njoku, E., Kellogg, K.: The NASA soil moisture active passive (SMAP) mission: overview. In: IEEE International Geoscience and Remote Sensing Symposium, pp. 3236–3239 (2010)
19. Yang, K., Shahabi, C.: A PCA-based similarity measure for multivariate time series. In: Proceedings of the 2nd ACM International Workshop on Multimedia databases, pp. 65–74 (2004)
20. Lin, S., Clark, R., Birke, R., Schönborn, S., Trigoni, N., Roberts, S.: Anomaly detection for time series using vae lstm hybrid model. In: ICASSP 2020–2020 IEEE International Conference on Acoustics, Speech and Signal Processing (ICASSP), pp. 4322–4326 (2020)
21. Zhao, Y., Nasrullah, Z., Li, Z.: Pyod: a python toolbox for scalable outlier detection. arXiv:1901.01588 (2019)

Author Index

Printed in the United States
by Baker & Taylor Publisher Services

Printed in the United States
by Baker & Taylor Publisher Services